# angel day turning

by
greg thompson
&
donal mcgraith

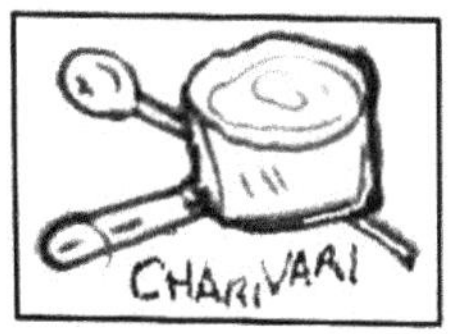

Canadian Cataloguing in Publication Data

McGraith, Donal & Thompson, Greg
Angel Day Turning

978-1-895166-17-0
1. Art. I. Title.
Printed and bound in North America.
First published 2021


Published by Charivari
87 Franklin Street,
Uxbridge, ON L9P 1J5

http://www.spoolmusic.com/charivari-home.html
https://charivaripress.news.blog

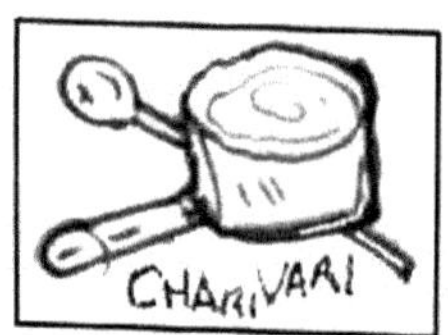

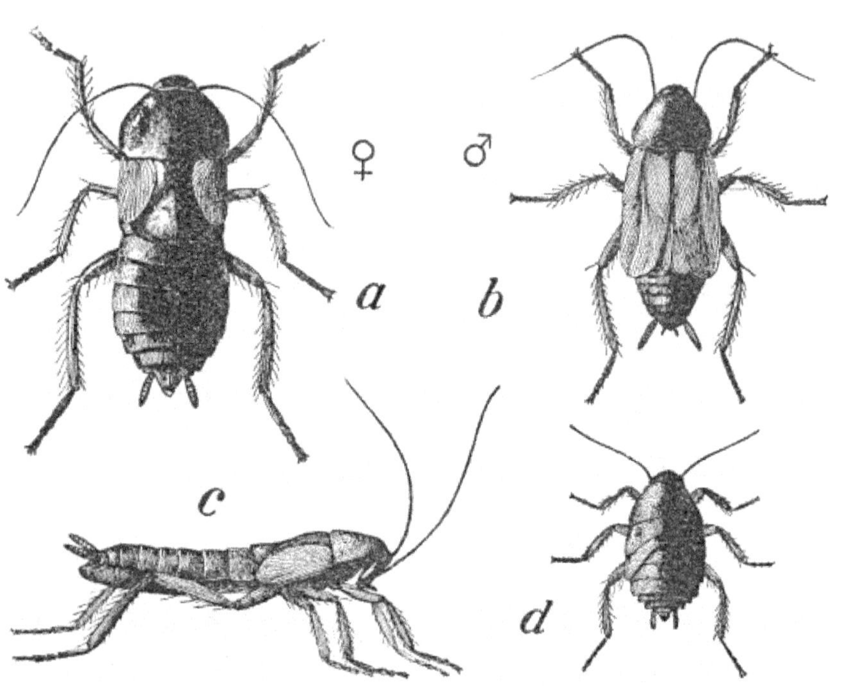
♀
♂
a
b
c
d

"… that which was previously mentally projected, which was lived as a metaphor in the terrestrial habitat is from now on projected, entirely without metaphor, into the absolute space of simulation."

—Jean Baudrillard

# Biervisitation.

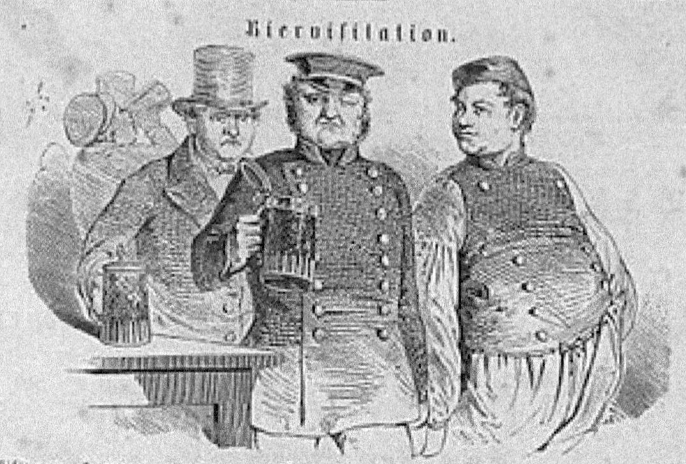

Visitator: I woaß net — i woaß net — das Bier hat an Geschmack — an Geschmack —
Wirth (drückt ihm heimlich einen Kronenthaler in die Hand).

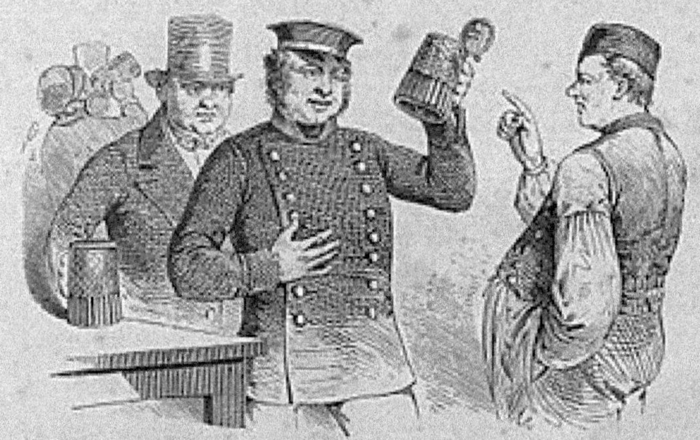

Visitator (mit Ausdruck): — an Geschmack — aber was für'n Geschmack! An'n ausgezeichneten Geschmack!

Angels are reification, the
anthropomorphisation
of value.

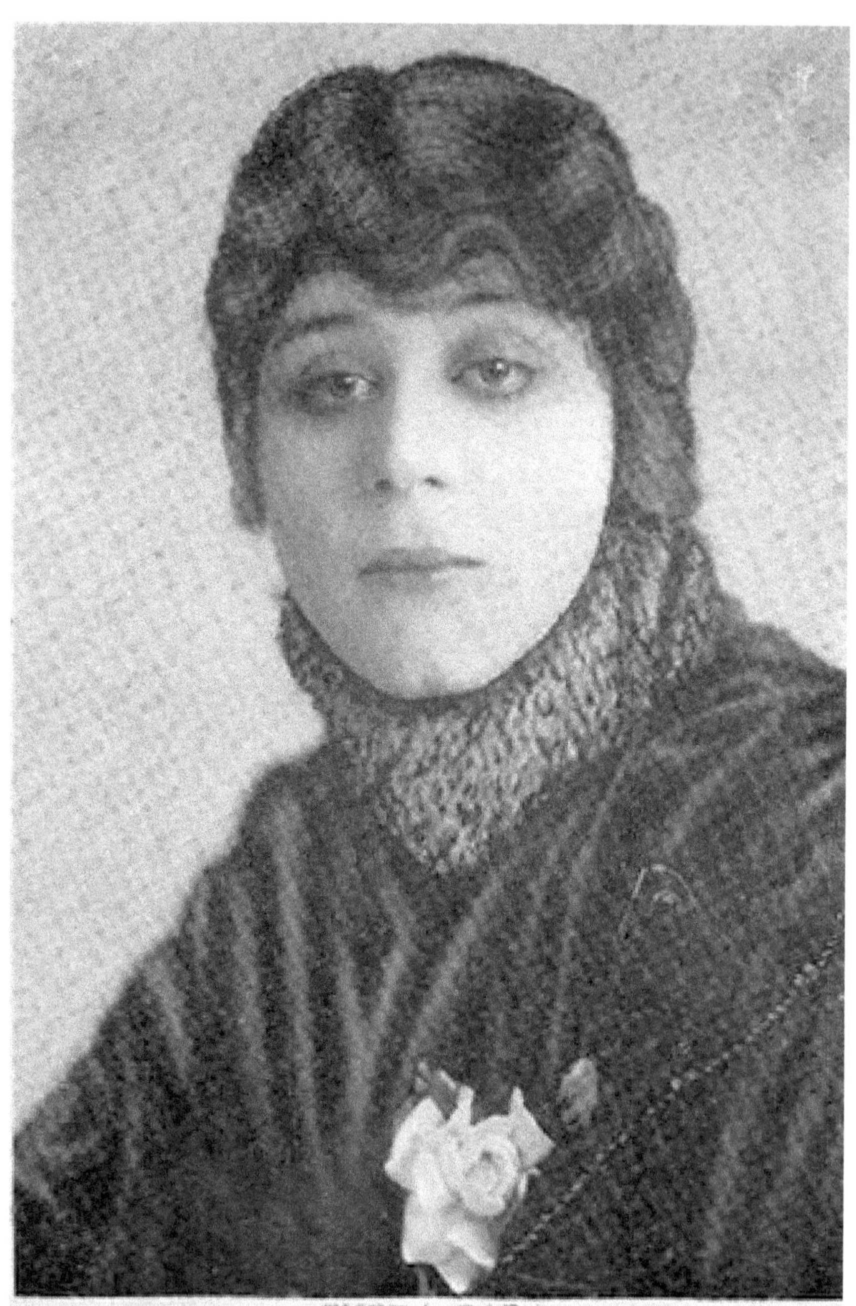

THEDA BARA

To track the traces of the incorporeal, both benevolent and malevolent, amongst the din of power transmissions emanating from the skies, I try to isolate the voices and apparitions that appear to sound momentarily on the dream screen before they fly away. I want to capture the angel and make it work for my desires without tricking me or slaying me or immobilizing me in my lust, greed, sloth, vanity, et cetera. The voice of the messengers of God is the media.

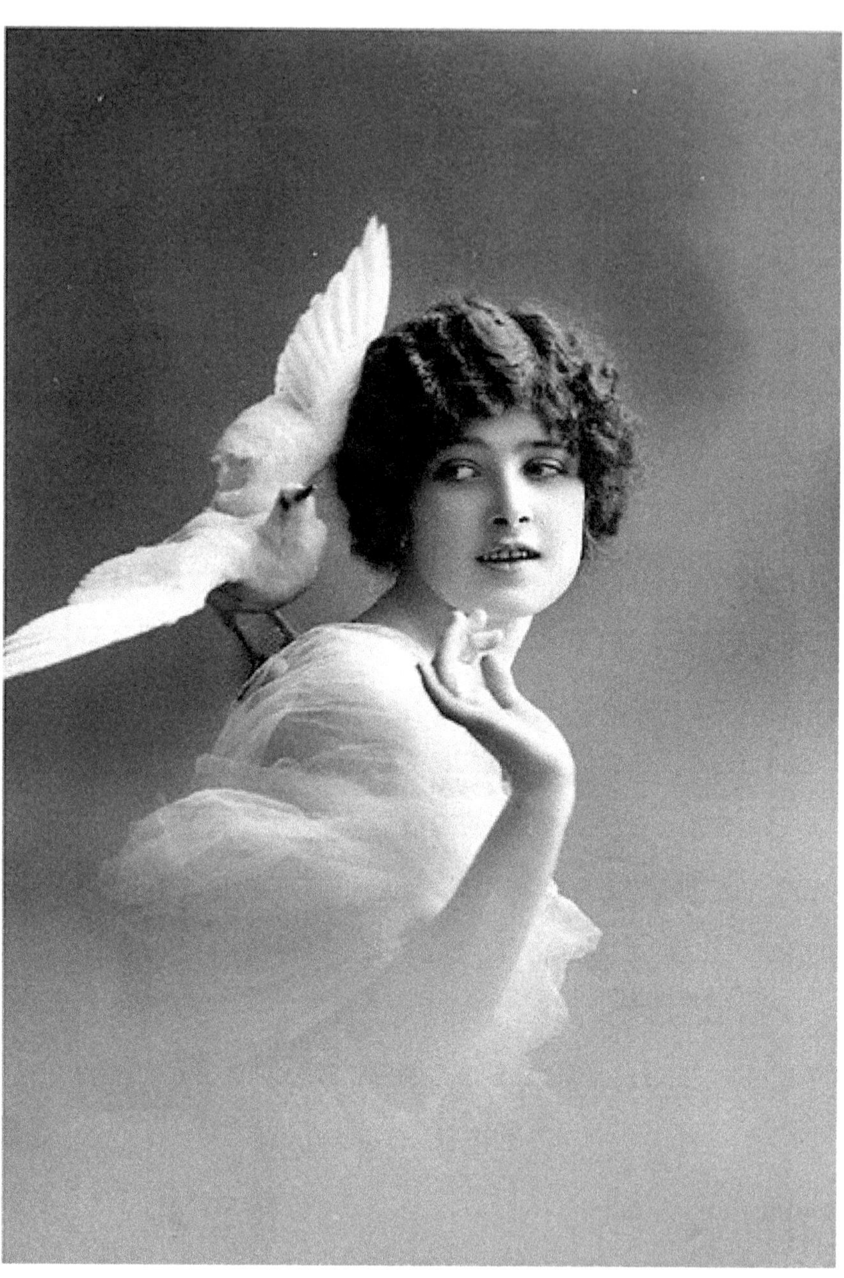

We are all fakes, made in the image of god, a transgression in itself, inauthentic, plagiarized like the Bible. If we are vehicles of her word then there is no authenticity, no original idea except that of her.

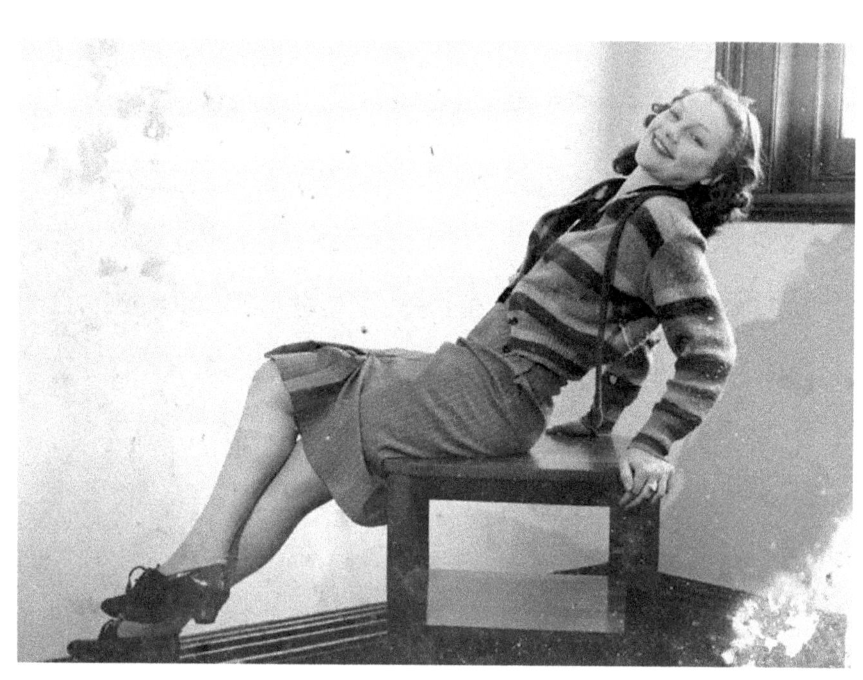

An angel is our idea of a more authentic (incorporeal) image of us, a pure soul never embodied, a contradiction, the mirror phase, our truer self then image. Angels are beauty that is skin deep, the glamour of the body without the actually desiring flesh – pure desire unfulfillable.

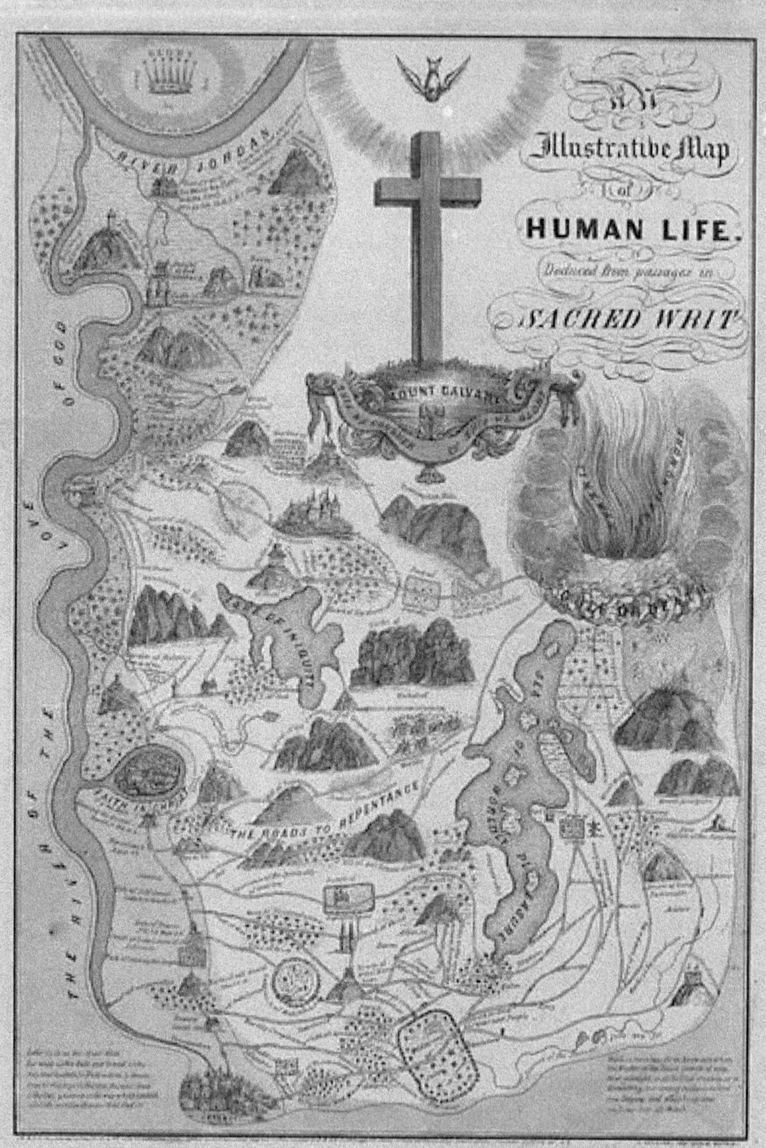
Illustrative Map
of
HUMAN LIFE.
Deduced from passages in
SACRED WRIT
RIVER JORDAN
MOUNT CALVARY
THE RIVER OF THE LOVE OF GOD
LAKE OF INIQUITY
THE ROADS TO REPENTANCE

The glorious messengers of God's unattainable beauty is the star, the model, the artist, but more precisely their transmitted evanescent image, not their person. In fact, the star, the model, the artist are not persons.

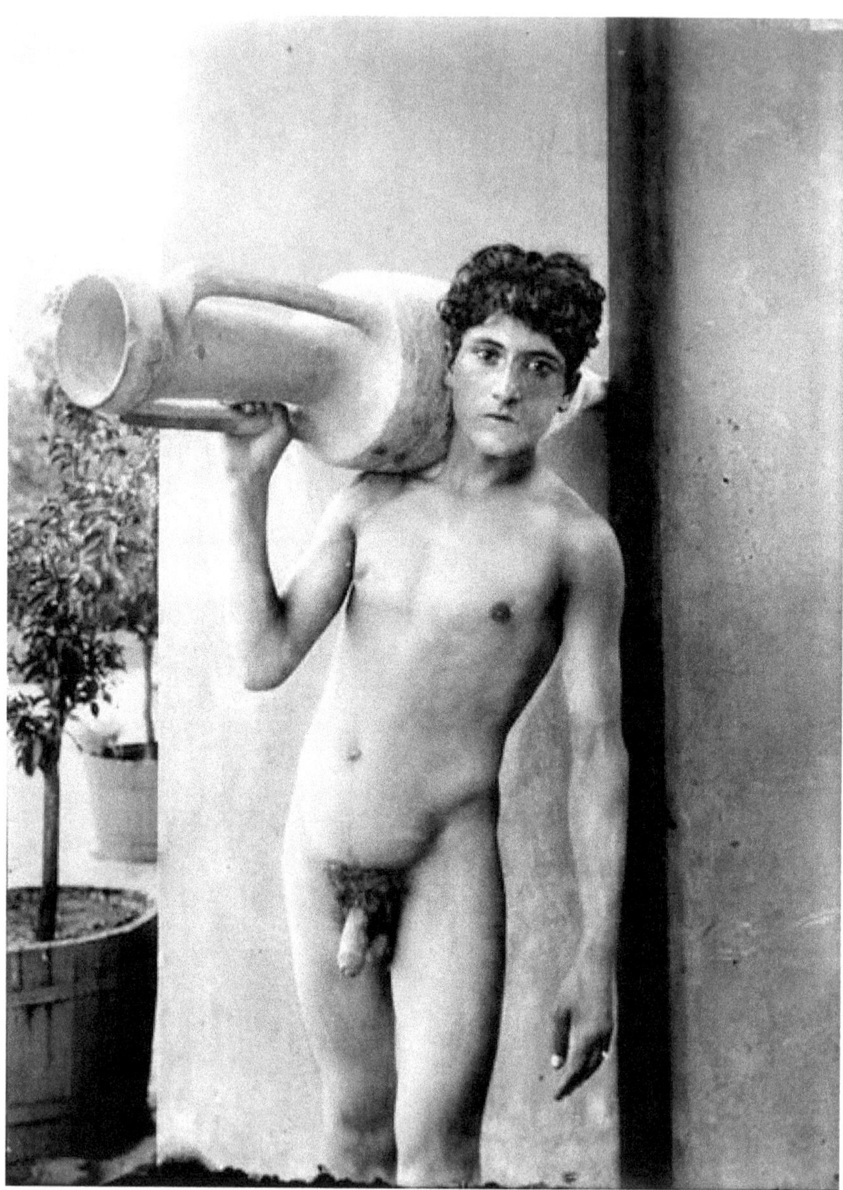

The Angel of Mercy, hope/
lassitude and the Angel of
Death, justice/revenge are
interventions of our dreams
into our everyday life where
our faith in fairness is
played out in a drama of
sympathetic magic.

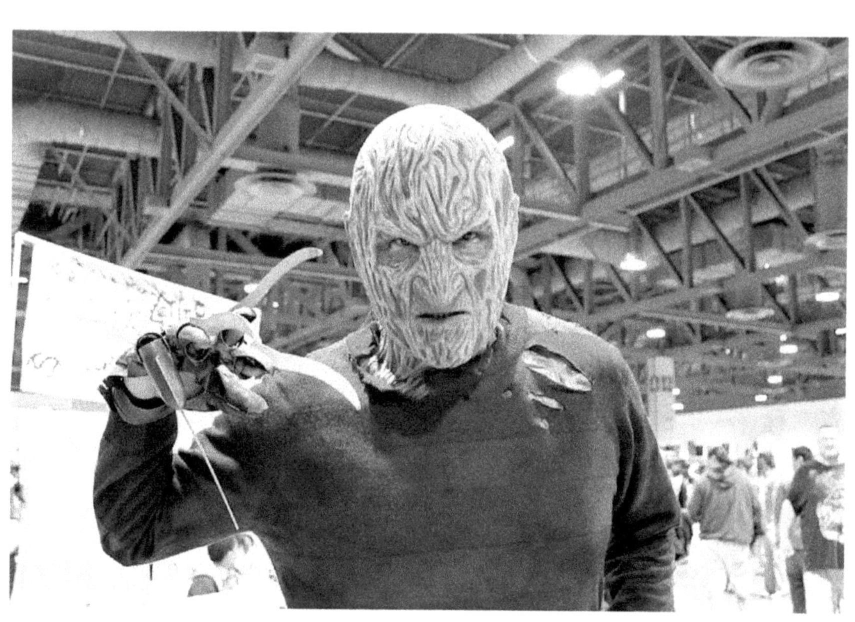

We cast a spell to save us from ourselves and punish all those perpetrators of evil we encounter in the misery of our everyday lives. Our Guardian Angels are vigilantes and thugs sent to expel our basest fears. The stories of angelic intervention make up our culture. Shane is an angel but so is Freddy Kreuger.

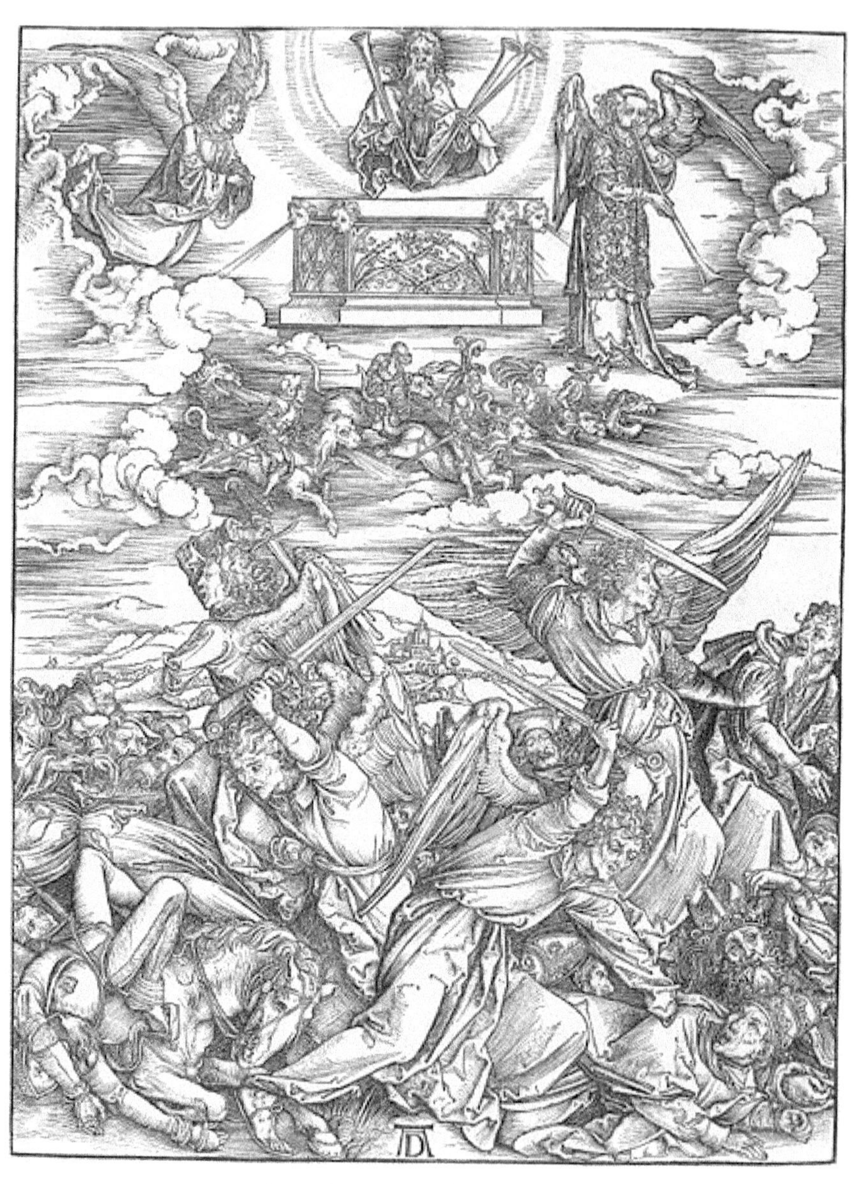

Albrecht Dürer (1471-1528)

It is necessary for angels
to be able to speak in all
languages, indeed all possible
languages, to show signs
that are understood in all
cultures. This presupposes
a metalanguage that contains
all language and culture. The
'existence' of angels requires
a Chomskyian deep structure.

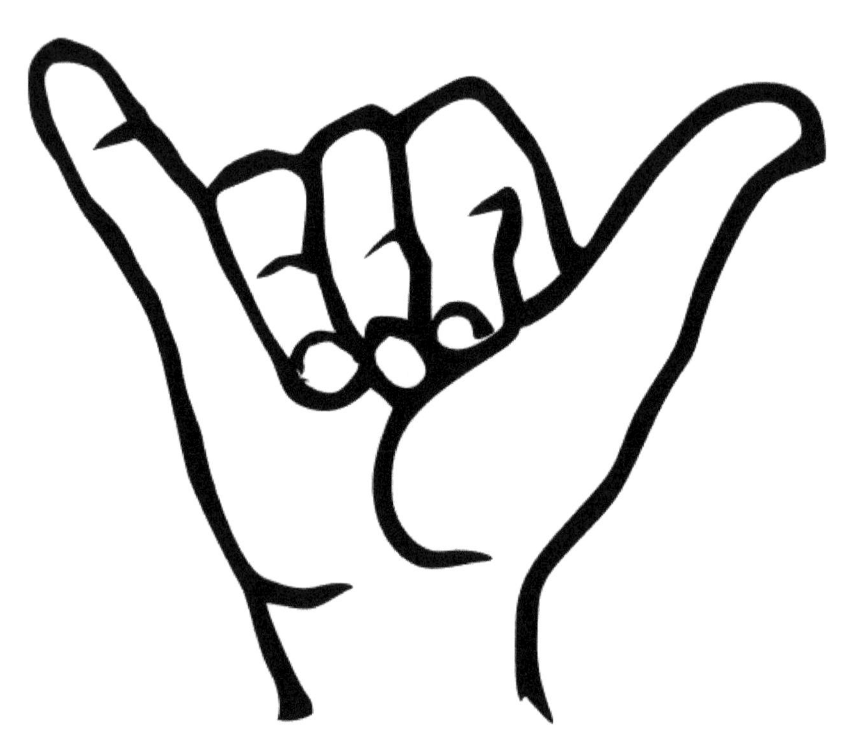

The easiest way to see this is to understand that the resurgence of angels is due to the ascendancy of binary code, the digital disassembly/ assembly of all culture for computer based distribution and control.

ISBN 978-1-895166-40-8
90000
9 781895 166408

Perhaps the existence of
a digital metalanguage
creates angels; angels being
simulation, disembodied power.

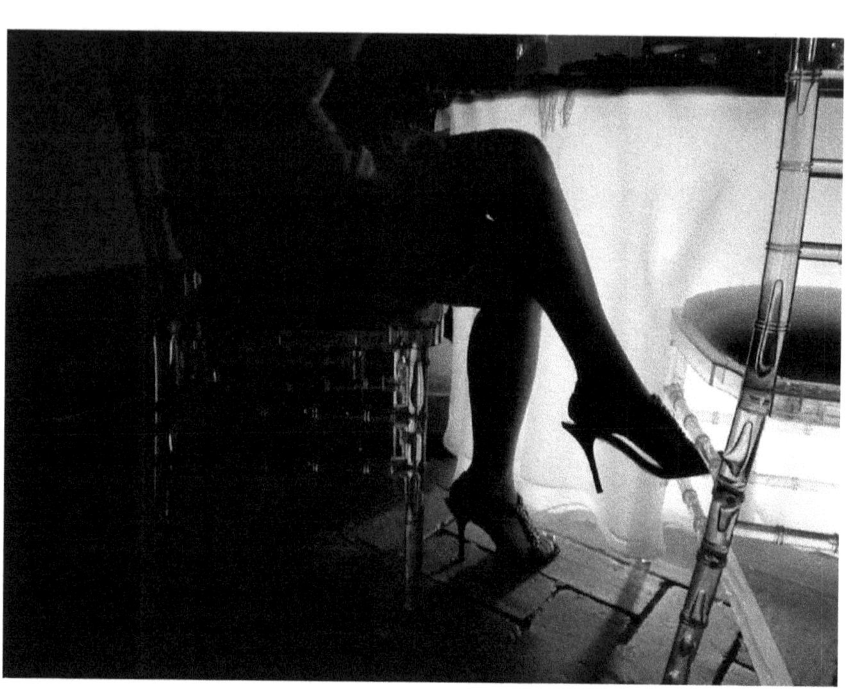

The historiography of art and culture represents itself as whole when in fact it is and has always been a sampling technique. A sampling technique unlike the digital in the sense that it does not try to comprehend the whole by eliminating mathematical redundancies but by editing and censoring for political and economic reasons.

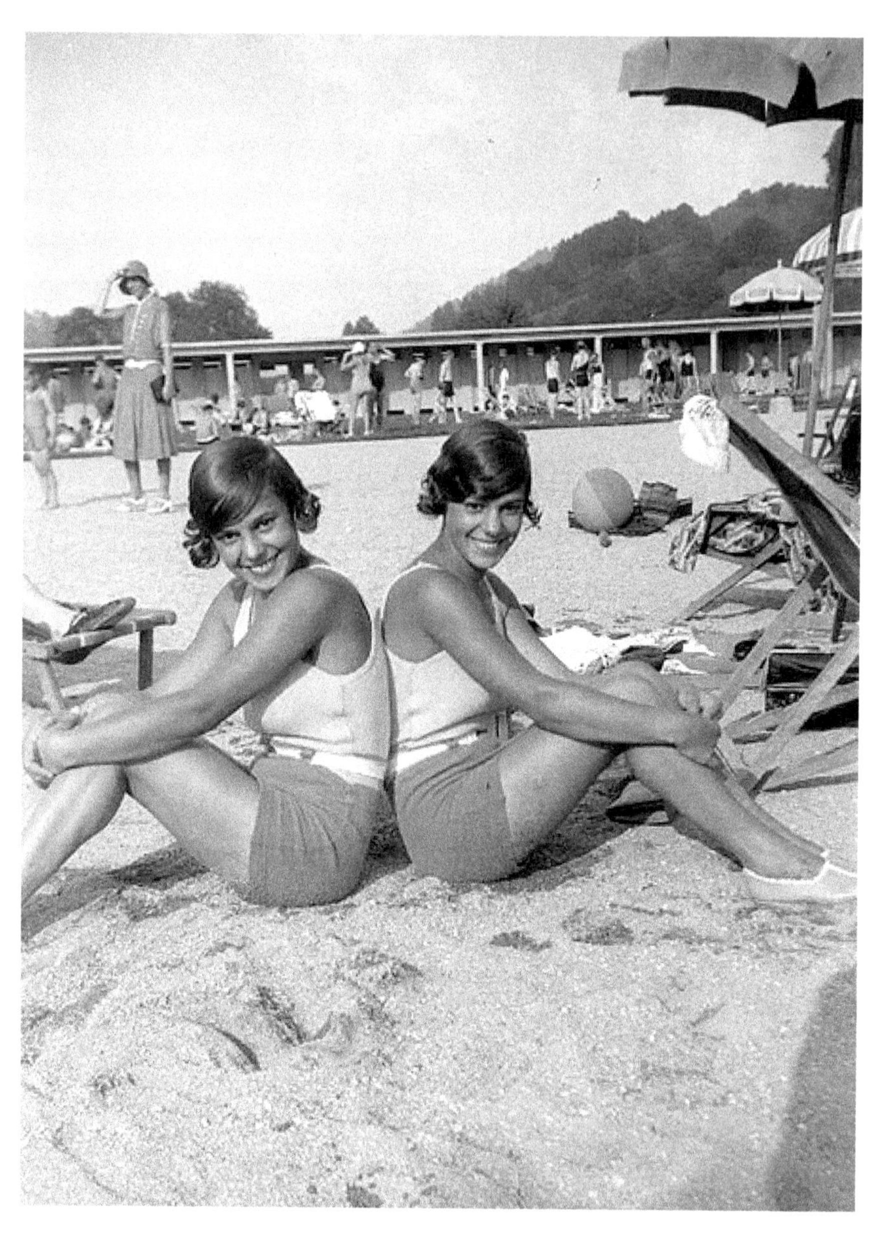

Originally Heaven and Hell were the same place. Until the late middle ages the personalities of angels slipped between good and evil. In a futile attempt to remove responsibility of evil from God, Heaven and Hell were separated and an attempt was made to separate good angels from demons.

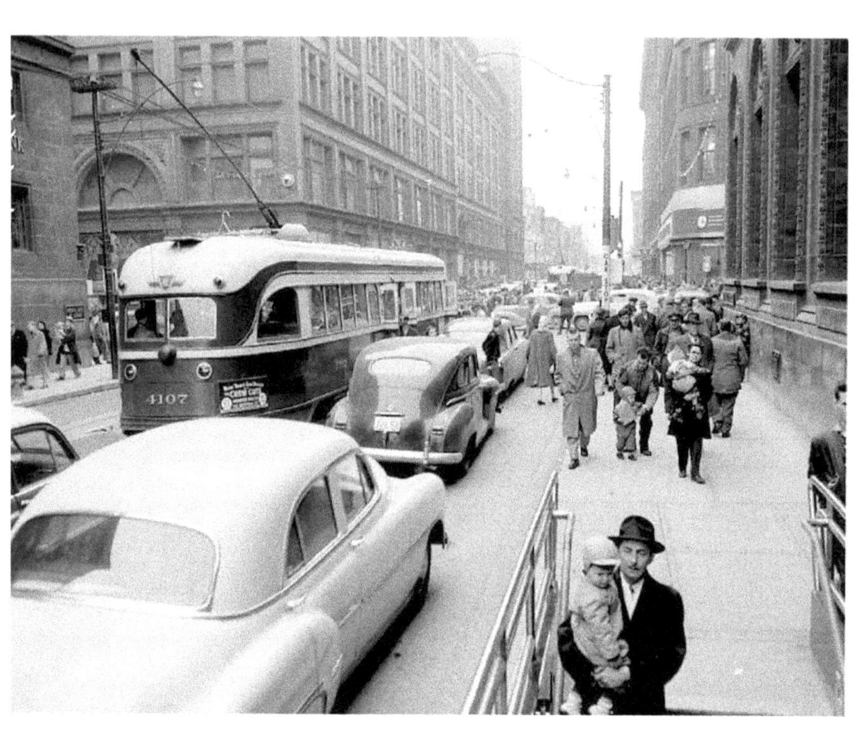
4107

This revision has never fully worked.

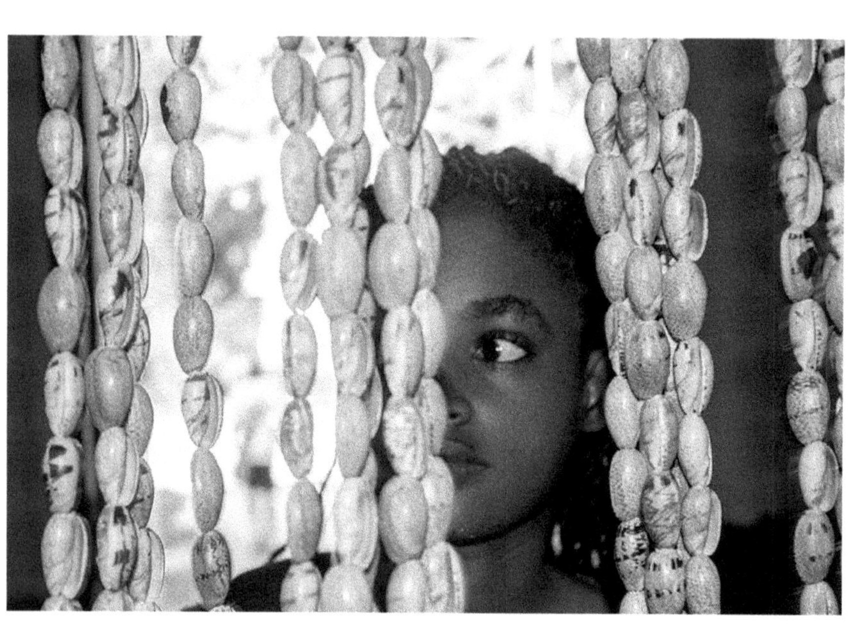

# Beauty

I thought she was beautiful,
but my thoughts were ugly.
I didn't want the image
of her but the flesh. This
intercourse spoiled her
beauty for me. I couldn't
reconcile my pleasure with her
beauty, which only existed
at a distance and seemed to
fade over time as I got to
know her. Maybe my pleasure
increased, but my desire for
that beauty declined.

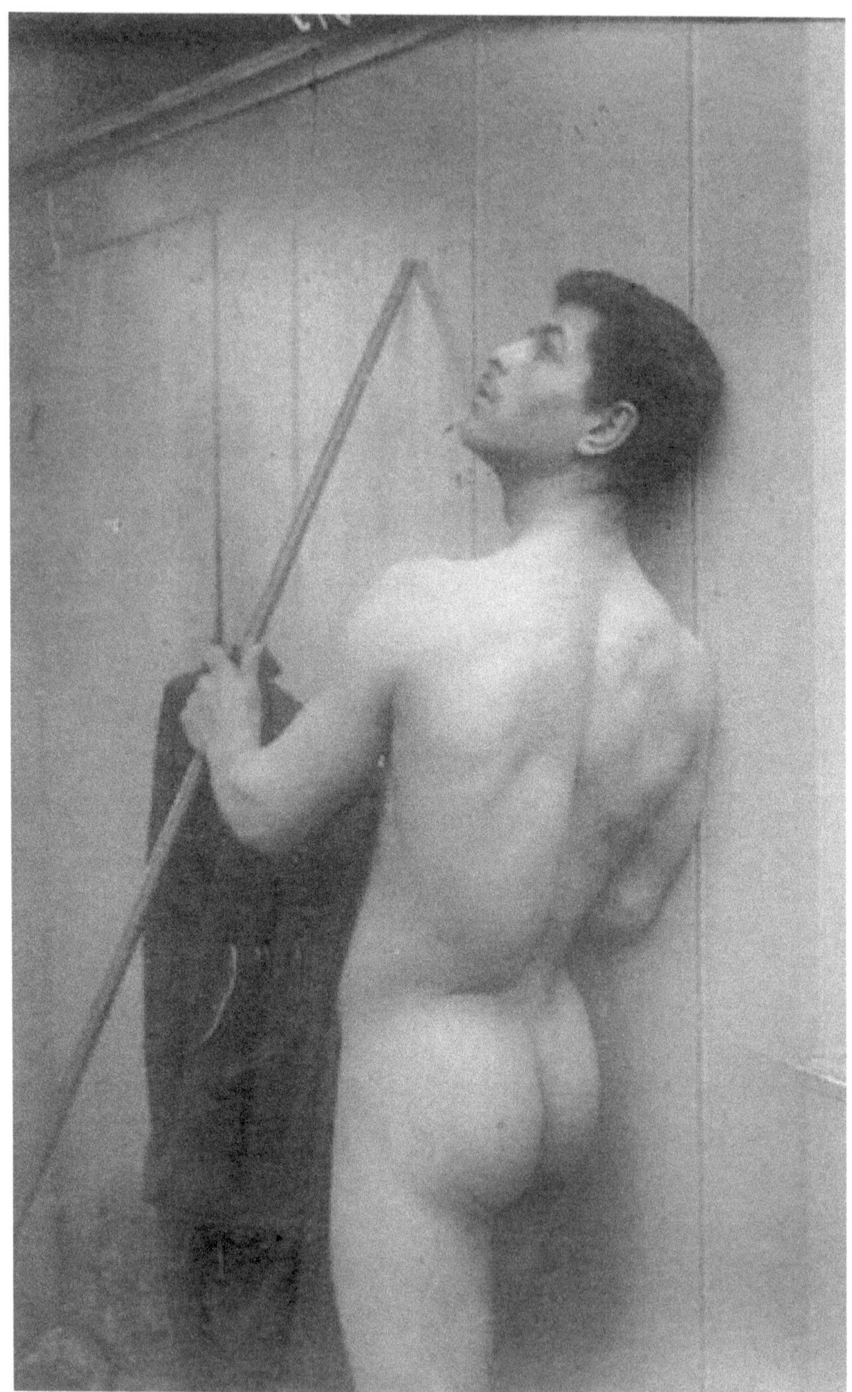

Beauty seems to be bodily
when in fact it is heavenly.
The beauty of any thing
is based on the beauty of
bodies, sexual attraction
sublimated into esoteric
clues (or codes). The beauty
experienced, an hormonal
hallucination, does not reside
in the body.

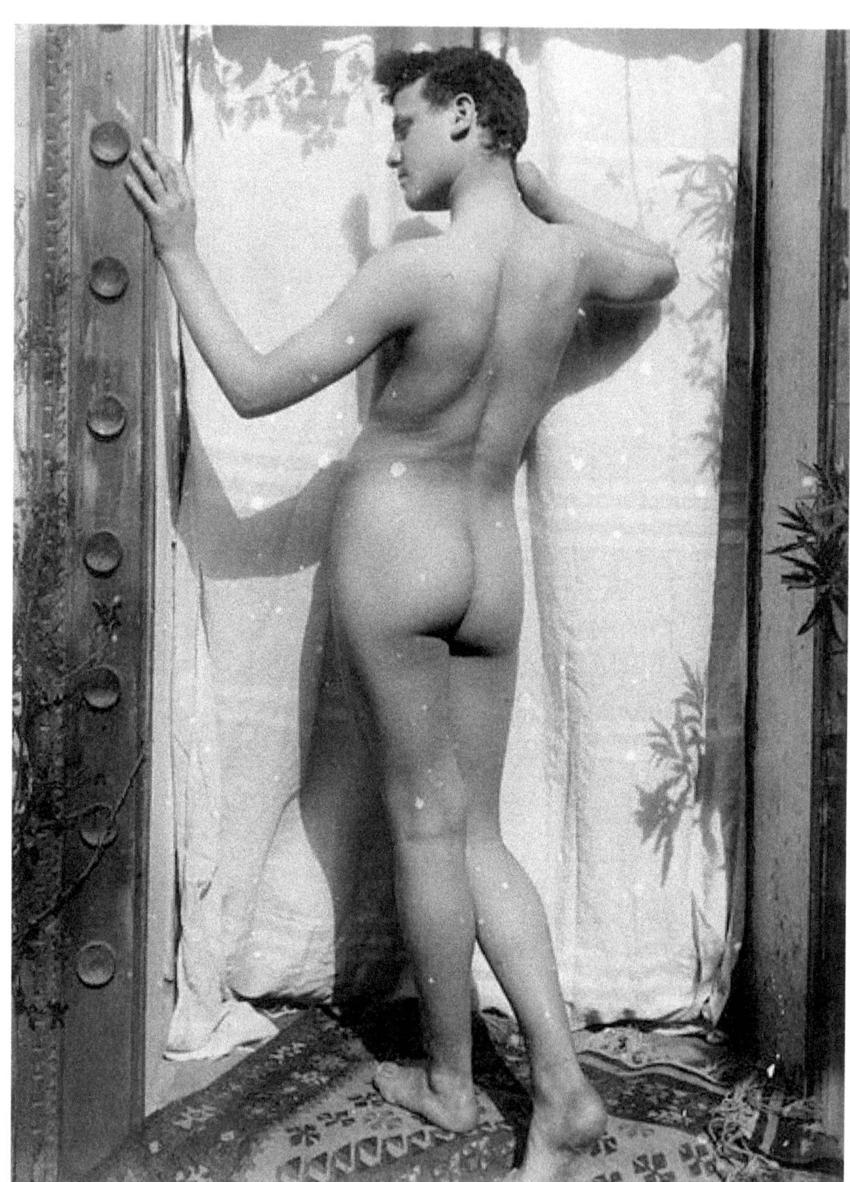

The normal functioning of the body is in opposition to beauty. The continual processing of this biochemical machine undermines any actual physical substructure for beauty. Beauty is fleeting. It exists extra-temporally, which is why it is best represented — as in a photograph, frozen, timeless.

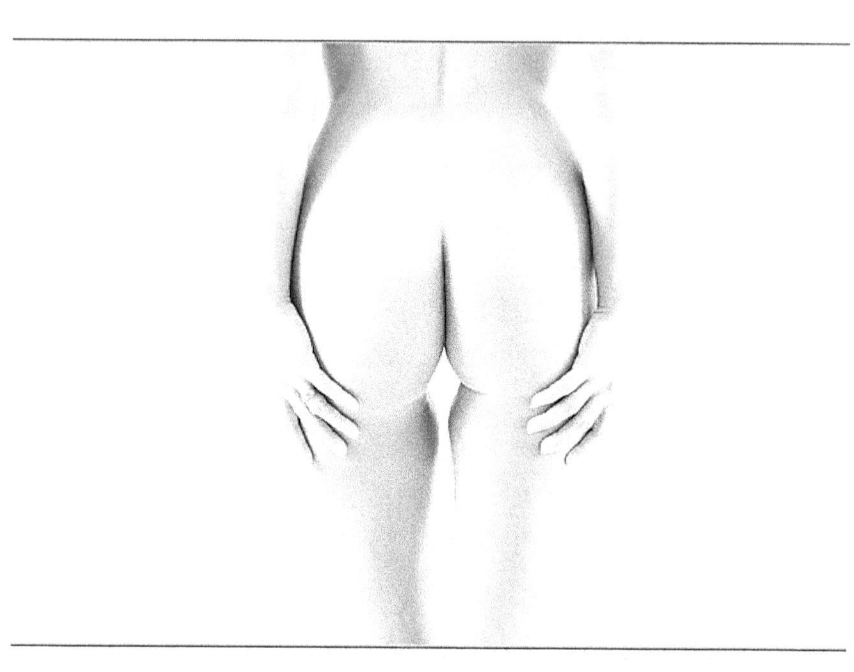

Beauty exists wholly outside the body of the model, a projection of lust. Beauty is an angelic feature precisely because of its very duplicity; precisely because it is not fair-minded but rather exclusive, shallow and vindictive.

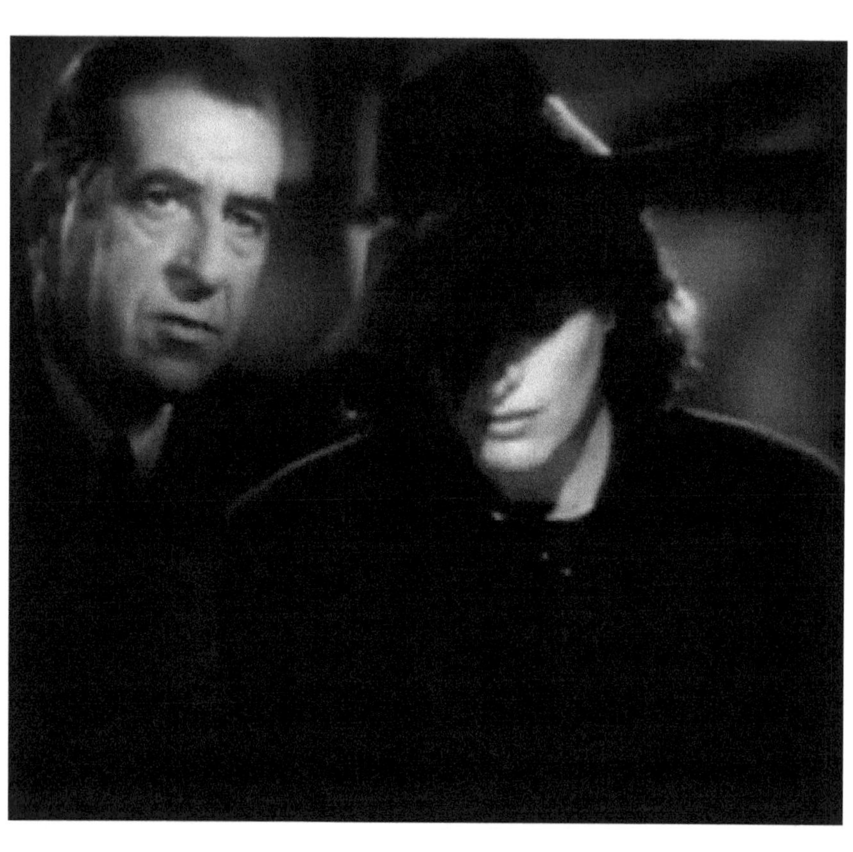

Though many want to say they find truth in beauty, they are lying to themselves. Beauty and truth are antithetical. Finding truth in beauty means substituting beauty for truth. Finding beauty in truth means being satisfied with easy solutions, it provides a reprieve from indeterminacy.

twist the head—move in straight lines. Apply more *Oatine* afterwards, the pores now being well opened, and finish by massage.

*No. 6.—A wrinkled face is a starved face.* Waste of tissue causes the lower skin tissue to contract and shrivel, leaving the outer covering like a loose mantle. To plump the tissues and eradicate wrinkles, apply *Oatine* with the finger tips until absorbed. Gently stroke the wrinkles crosswise with the tips of the fingers. Do this once a day for ten or fifteen minutes.

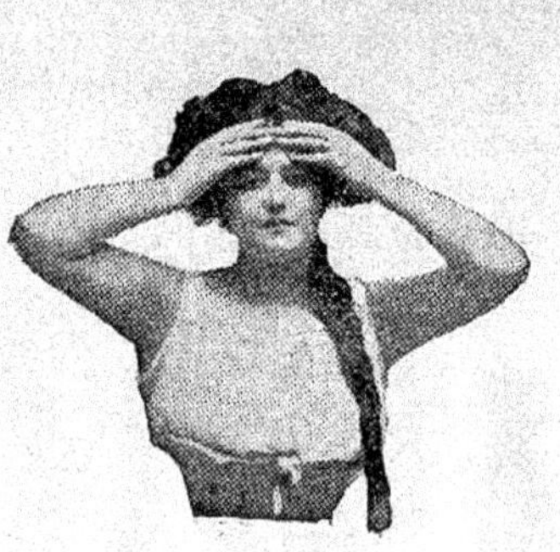

And this substitution, the domination of aesthetics, is a fundamental characteristic of a culture where the subjective is disguised as objective. Alternative definitions of beauty, cults of the ugly and passions for destruction all characterize their lust as transcendence.

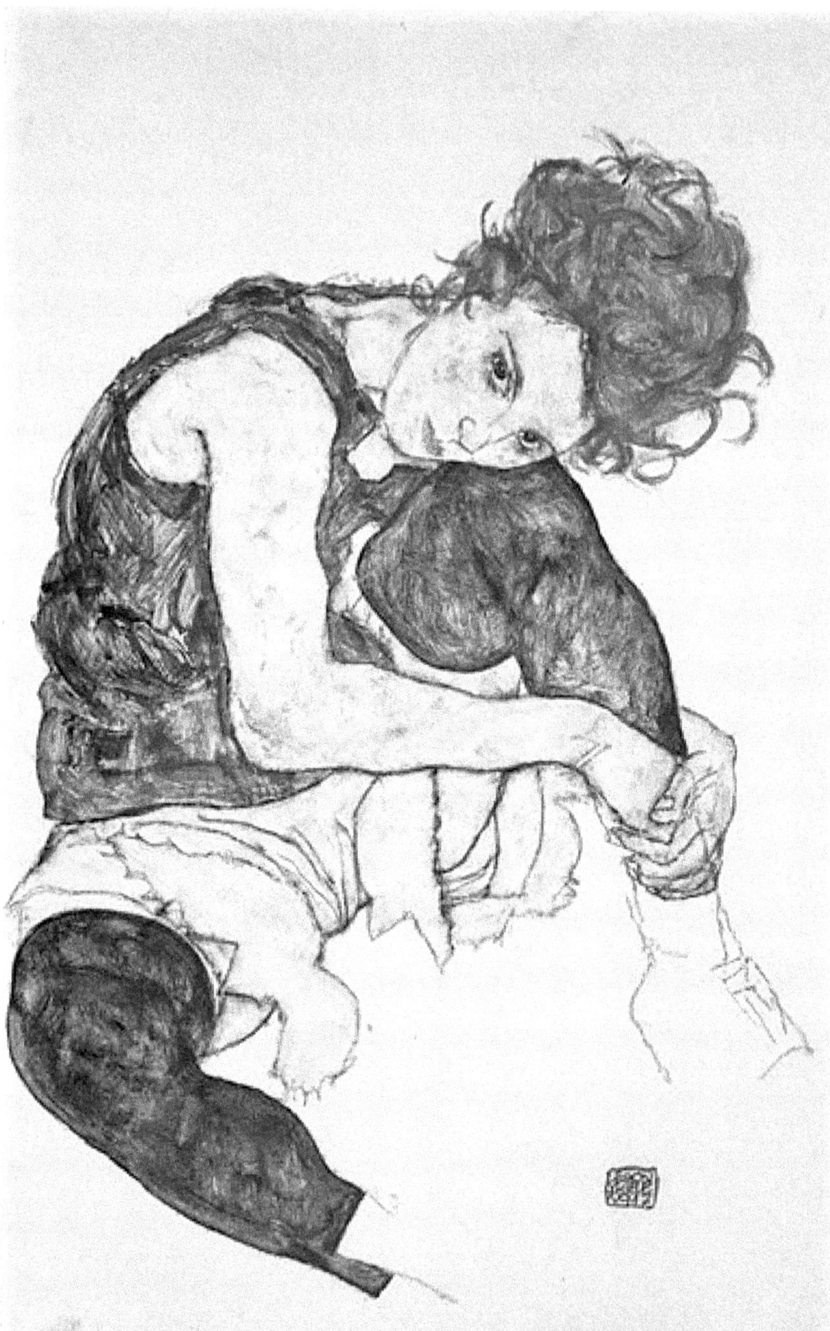

With the suppression of religious teleology by technological progress, the mechanisms of natural evolution become insufficient. In the realm of beauty, virtual reality has always existed. Beauty is a laboratory for technoevolution.

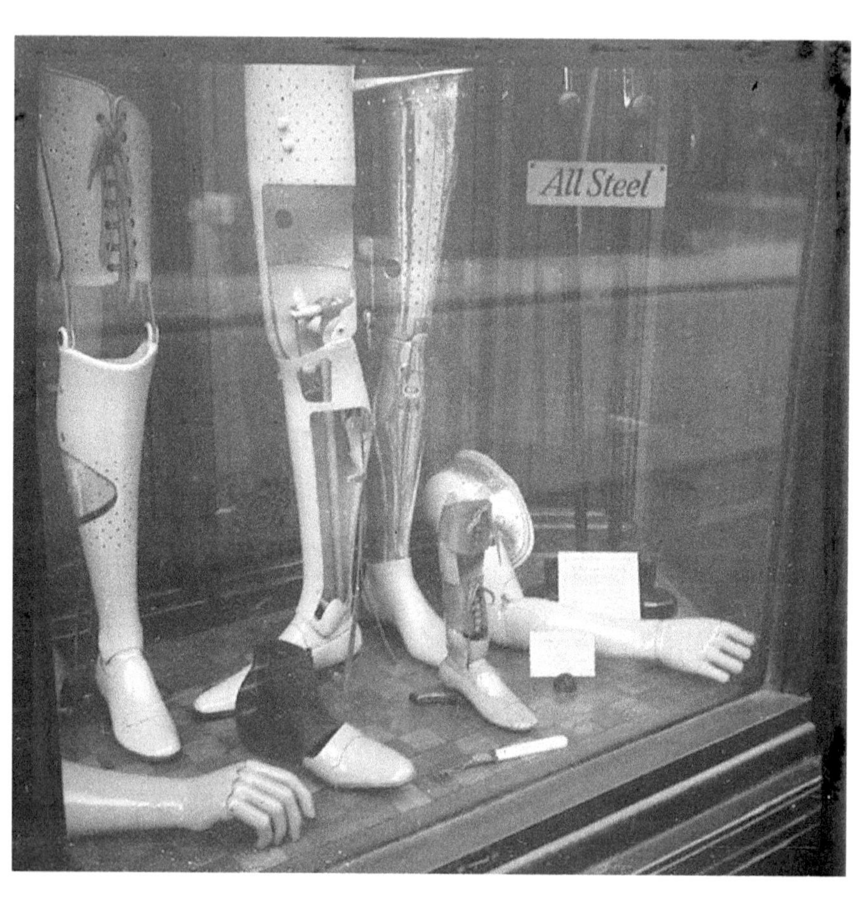
All Steel

There is the obvious, cosmetic surgery, prosthetic devices and body shaping machinery, but the real future of beauty resides in getting wired.

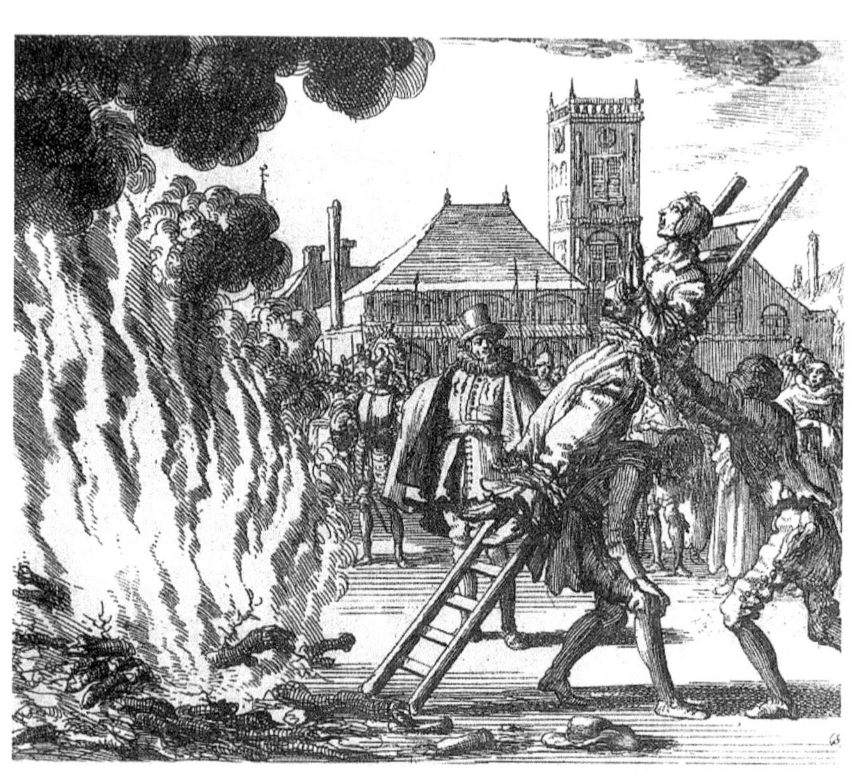

Rather than simply manipulating the biological structure of the human body's ecology in the digital world, we deal strictly with the image through instantaneous morphing. If one were to presume the absence of corruption we could see equal access to beauty both of the self and the other.

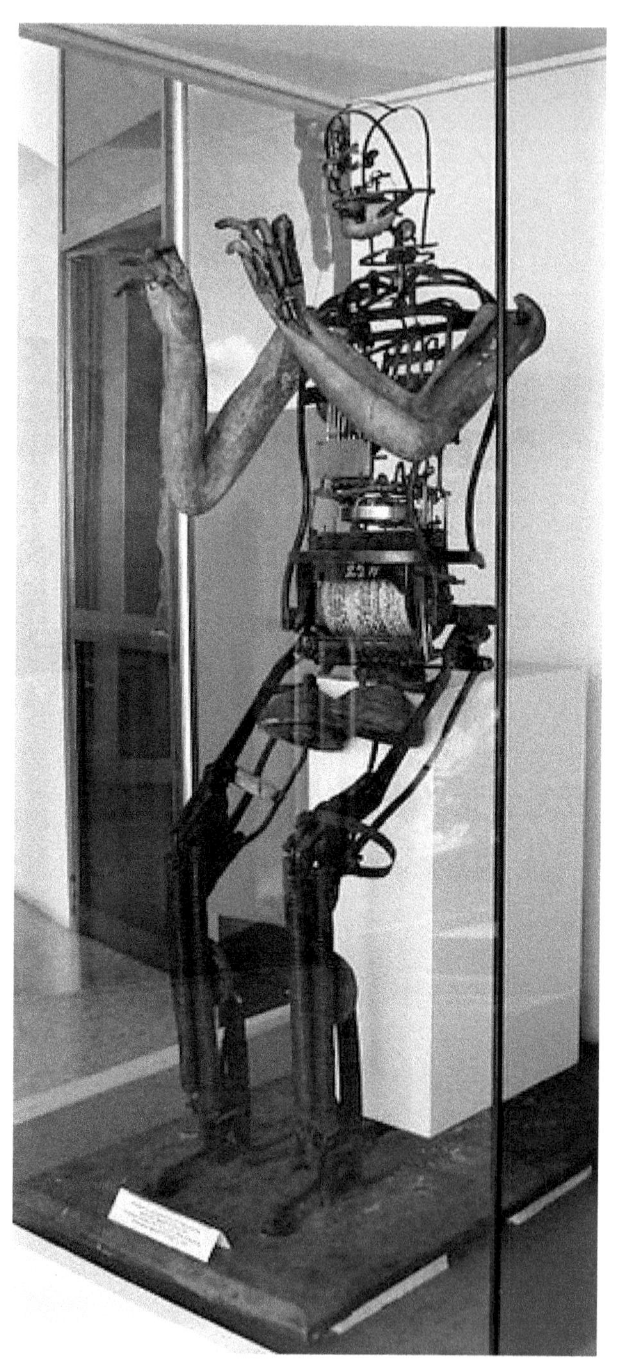

The angel is the body as pure transmission. The angel's body is not the machine, it is the projection of the machine. The angel is the body as pure transmission. The beauty of the angel lies in its lack of substance, its lack of bodily function, its lack of bodily fluids.

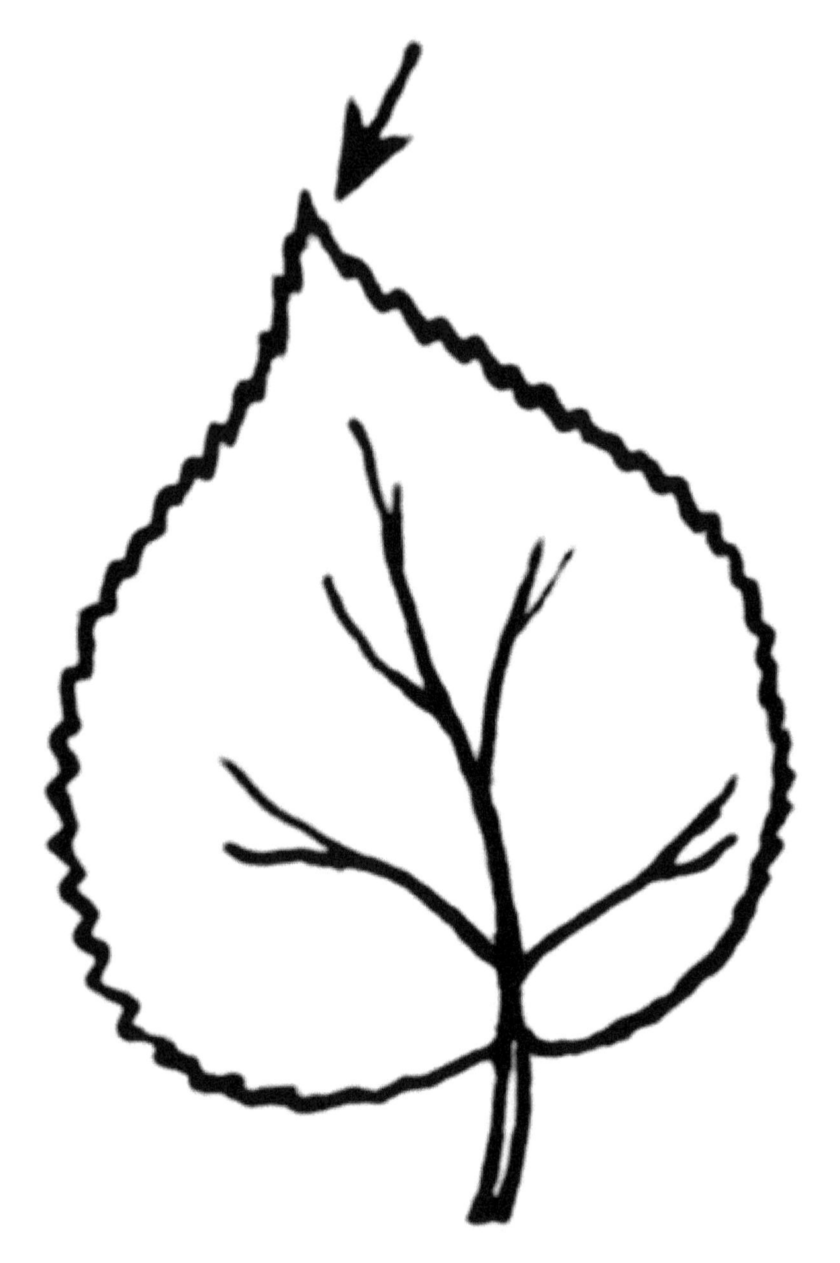

The angelic lies not in the actual technology but in how the technology projects the appearance of intent, of the self into vaporous simulation.

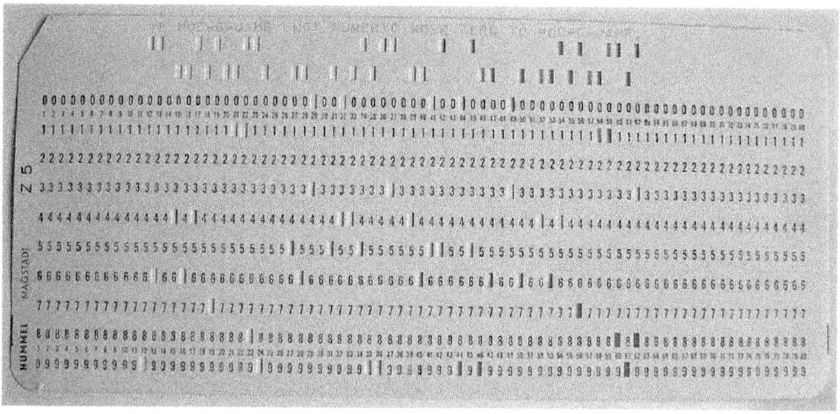

Beauty strives to leave the body and operate totally in the realm of the obscene, the brain, now hard wired to the network. The body rather than a self-regulating system of fluids becomes a fluid in yet another system. Bodies are exchanged and interchangeable in the fashion/media/beauty system.

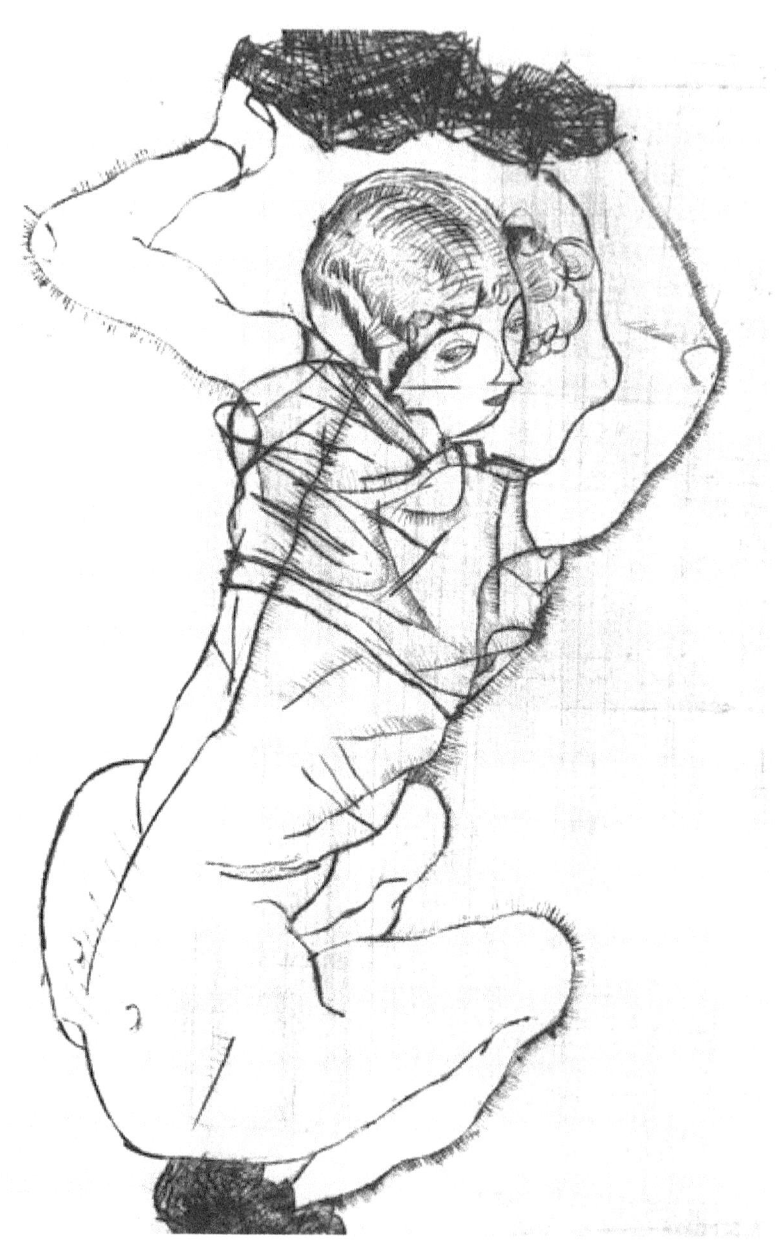

Beautiful bodies are not the seat of some person, the embodiment of mind. They belong apparently to corporations as the angelic image of the same; but ultimately the beautiful bodies belong to no one. The body is a component of a fluid, the ejaculate of the corporate.

PEOPLES GAS BUILDING, CHICAGO.

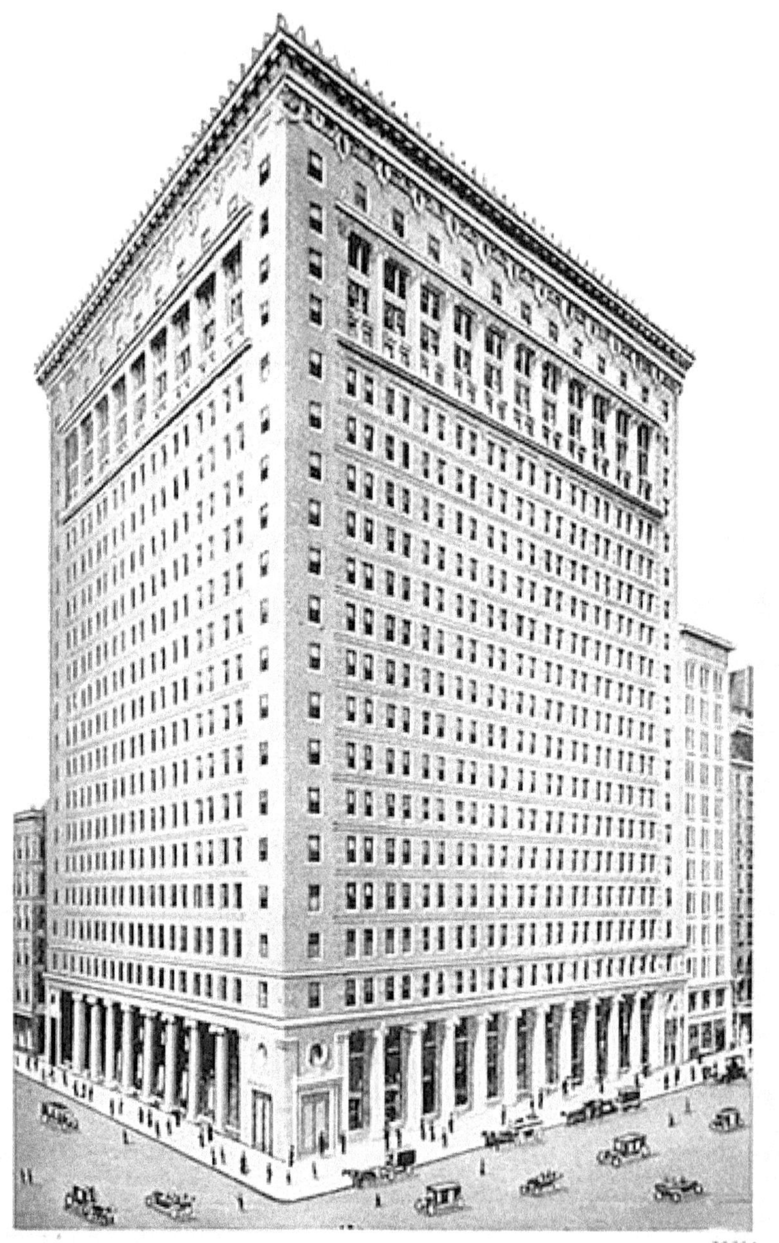

30204

# EVIL

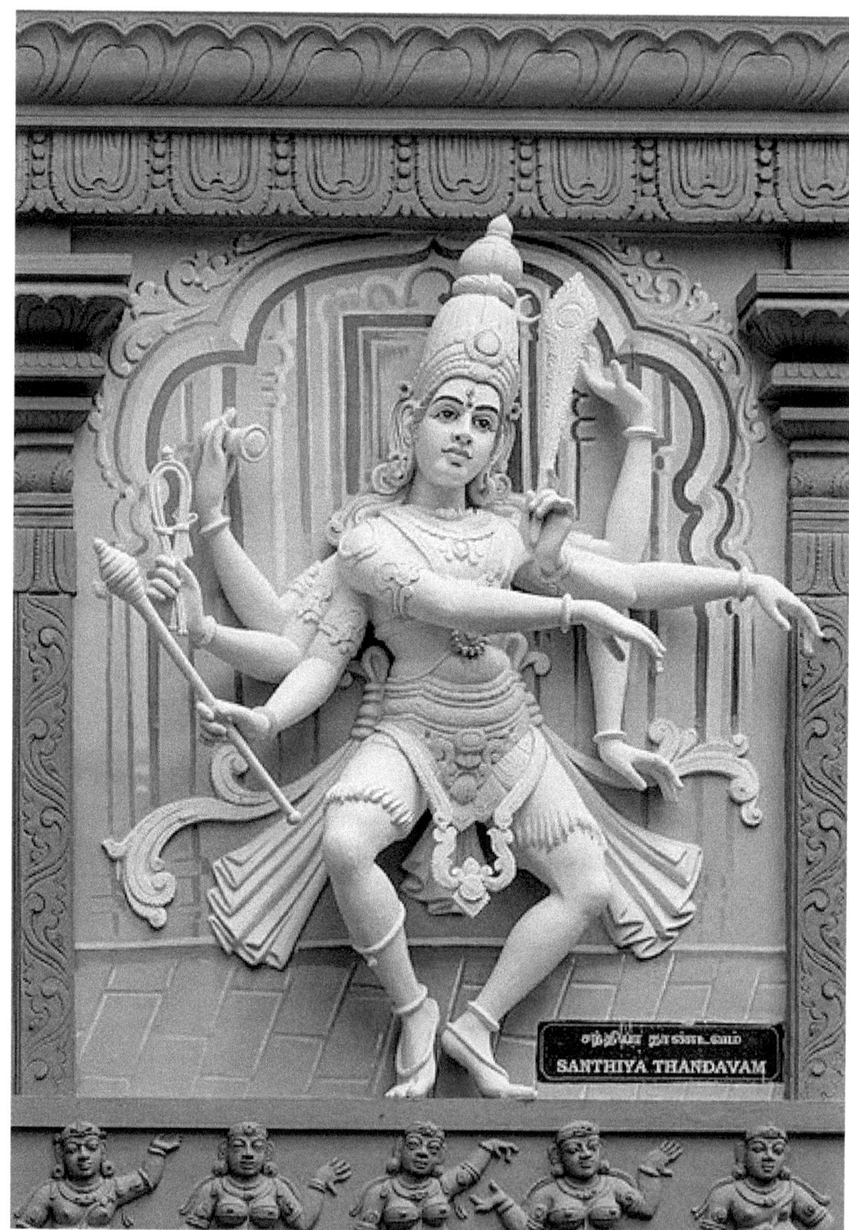
SANTHIYA THANDAVAM

Modernist culture with its predilection for holistic fantasies like art, ecology or politics is in denial. It is in denial about evil. In a rash of self-righteousness it postulates aesthetic and moral transcendencies.

# Puck

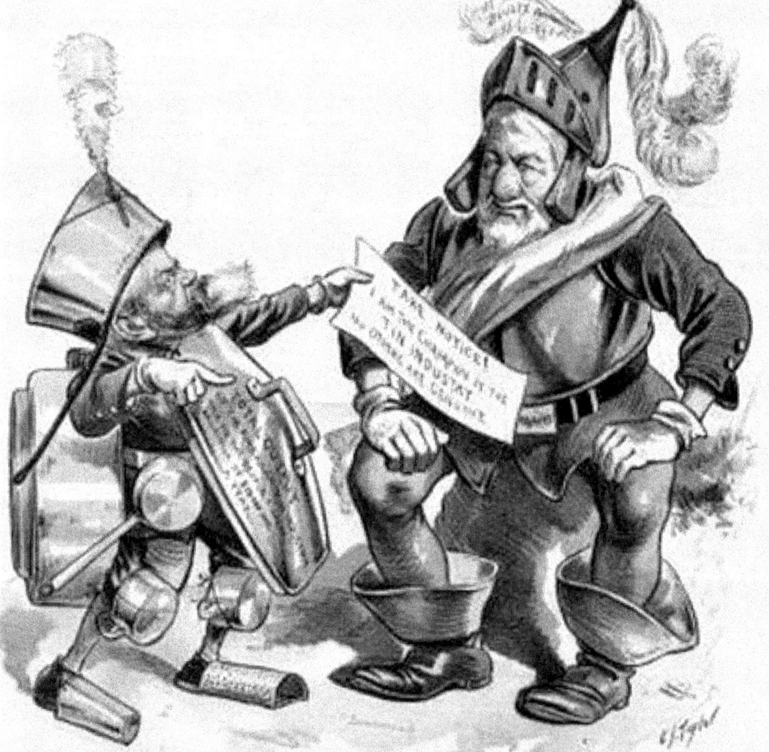


HE'S IN IT, TOO.

It tries to manipulate the reading of culture as a steady progression to utopia and in doing so melds the ultra-radical into the deeply reactionary.

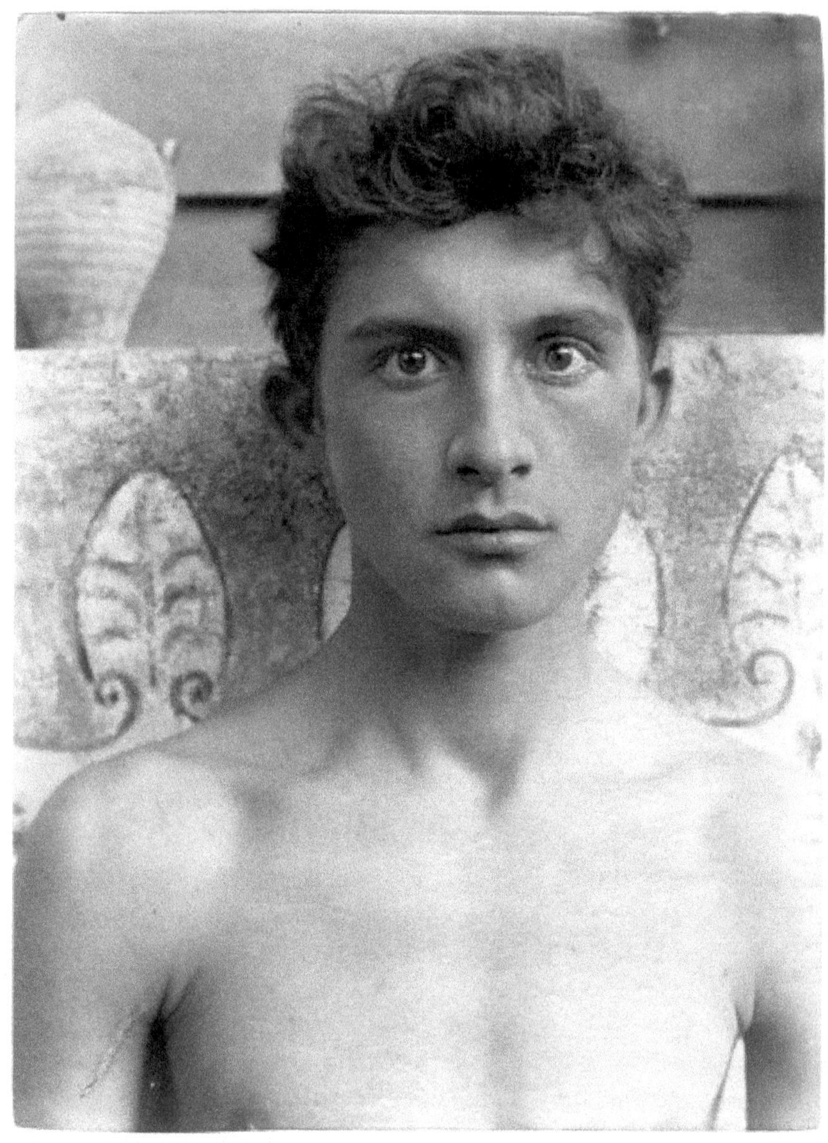

This wet dream of communism/ social democracy/progress elaborates the eradication of evil by tremendous benevolence of the social group and the technological supersession of hardship. The idea of crime becomes impossible in the face of personal and social fulfillment for all.

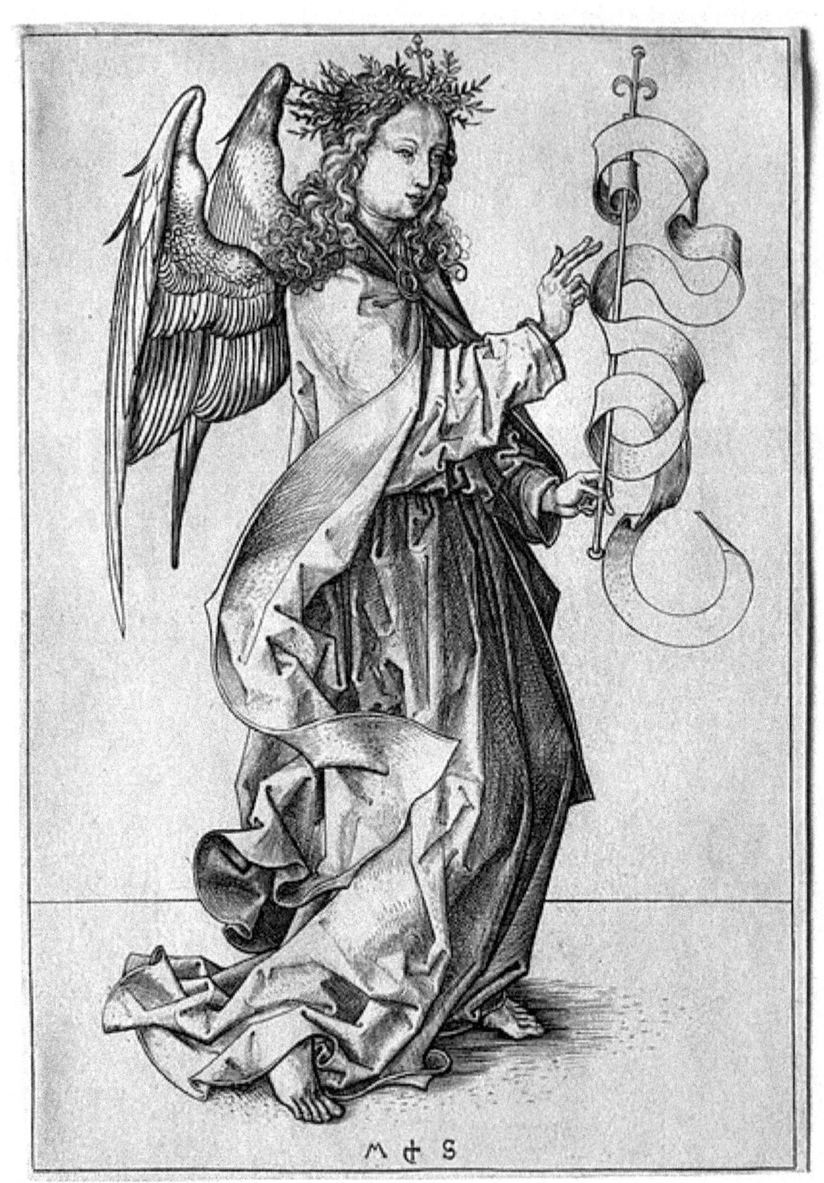

The socialist utopia or the myth of scientific progress supplanted the image of angels moving planets. This new machine is subject to the same degree of slippage as the theistic machine. Nothing really works the way it is supposed to.

She fought, she scratched, she pursued, she annoyed, she actually devilled the man into marrying her and she did it in a way that makes you glad she did and glad you can see her do it.

It's the kind of a picture you have come to expect from the name *Metro All Star Series Production* — and VIOLA DANA is absolutely fascinating as its star.

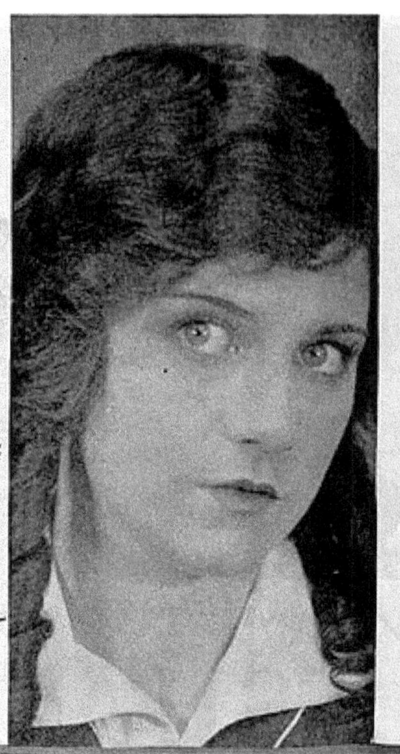

METRO PRESENTS

# VIOLA DANA

IN

# SATAN JUNIOR

*Adapted by John Collins from Vanzo Post's novel "Diana Ardway" published by the J.B. Lippencott Co. and directed by Herbert Blache.*

RELEASED BY METRO MARCH 3rd

MAXWELL KARGER, DIRECTOR GENERAL

Evil does exist. It doesn’t really matter whether the existence of evil is a conspiracy or that it is merely a synergy of self-interest or even an instinct for self-destruction. Angels represent a desire for a subjective moral order to be inflicted upon others but ascribed with consensus and/or objectivity.

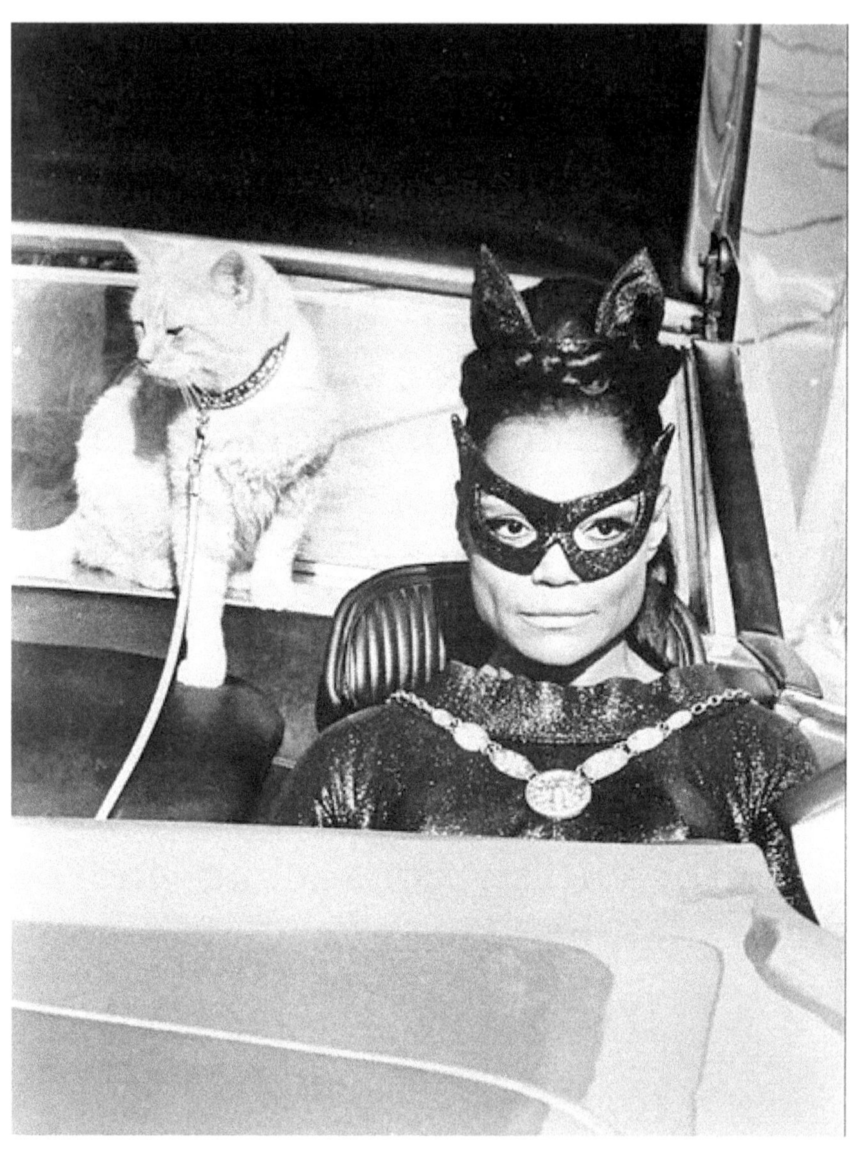

An angel is summoned to balance the books, for every moral debit there is a credit: to honour and relieve our suffering; to punish those who transgress against us; to fulfill our desires.

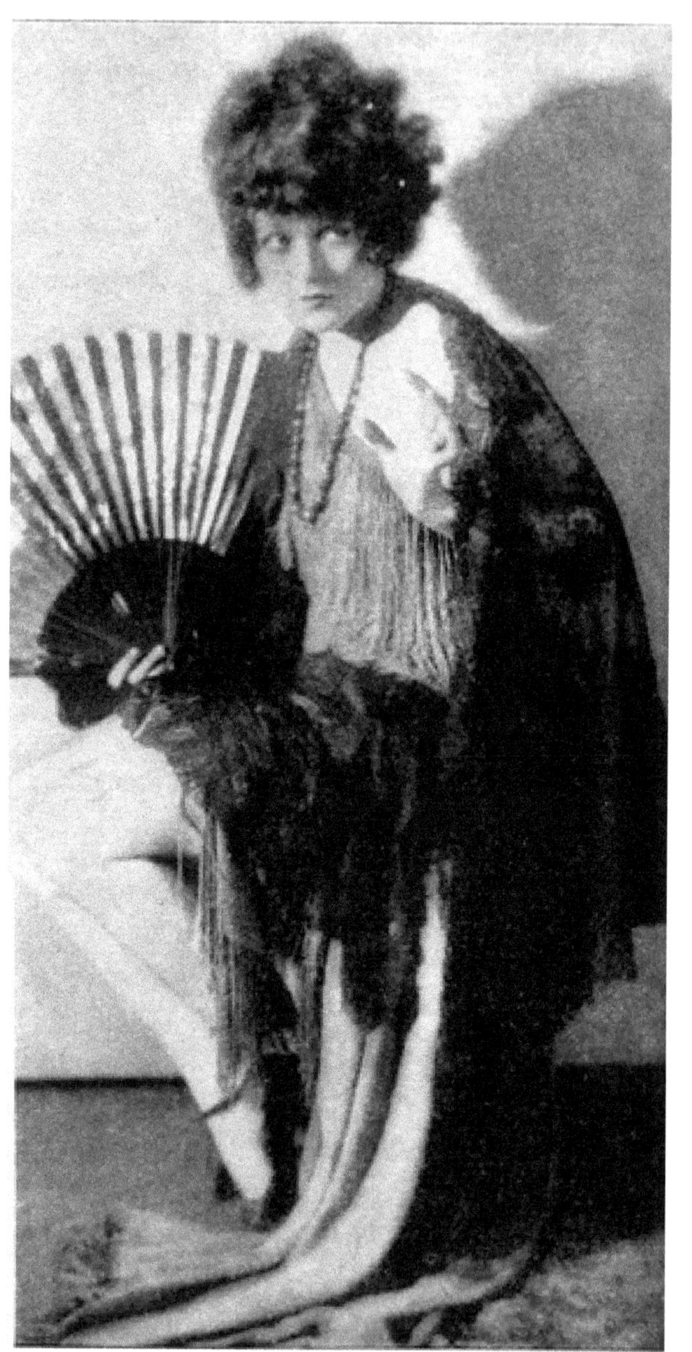

The angel represents our pitiful belief that those who abuse us will eventually get their just desserts and that we will be rewarded for all our good work and perseverance. Why do people believe this shit?

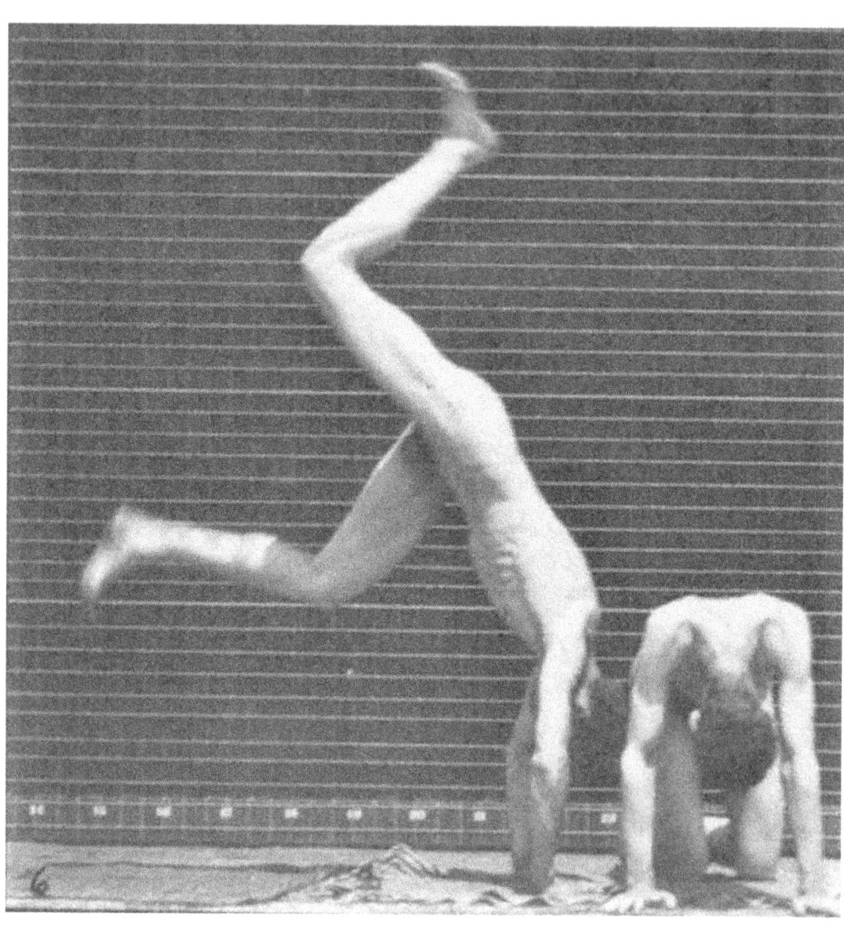

Perhaps the reality of evil is intolerable.

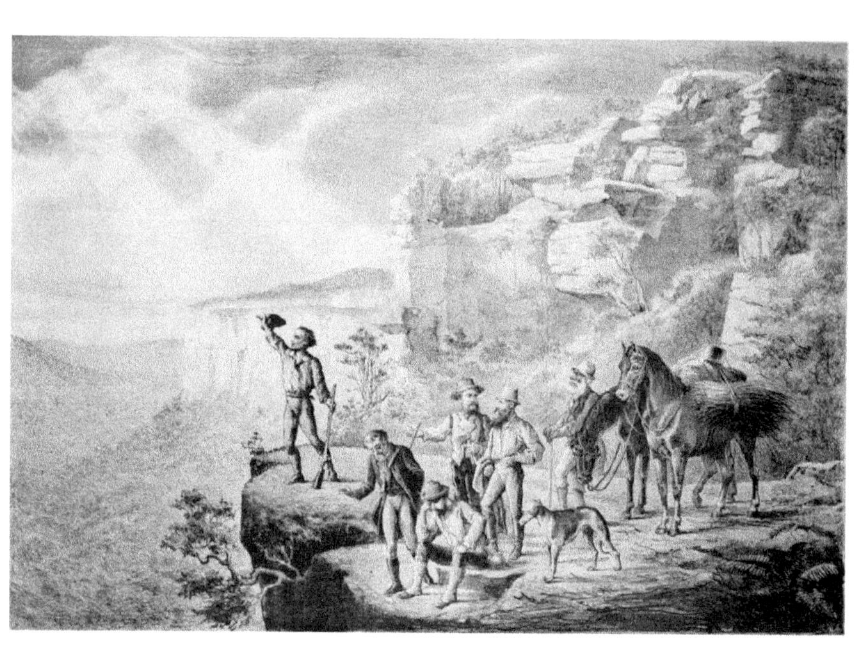

# HOPE

"If you wish upon a star..." —Clifton Avon Edwards.

"Hope is the leash of submission." —Raoul Vaneigem.

"They will lean that way forever." —Leonard Cohen.

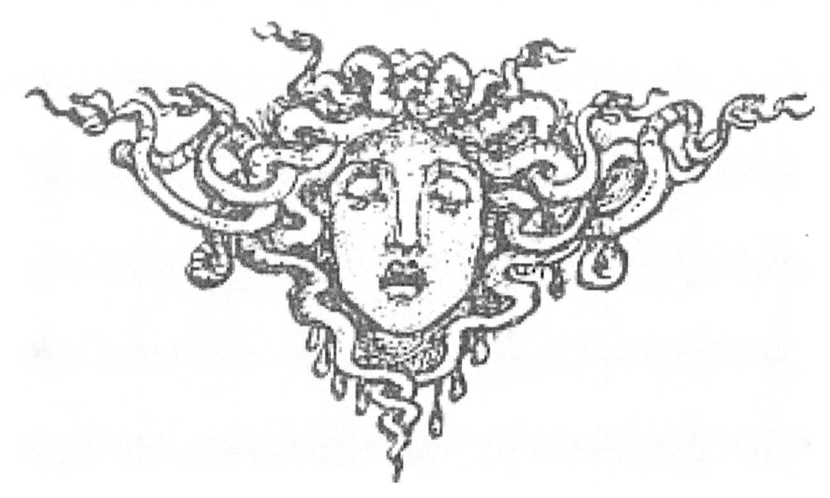

The more powerless we become the more frequent the sightings of cybernetic poltergeists become.

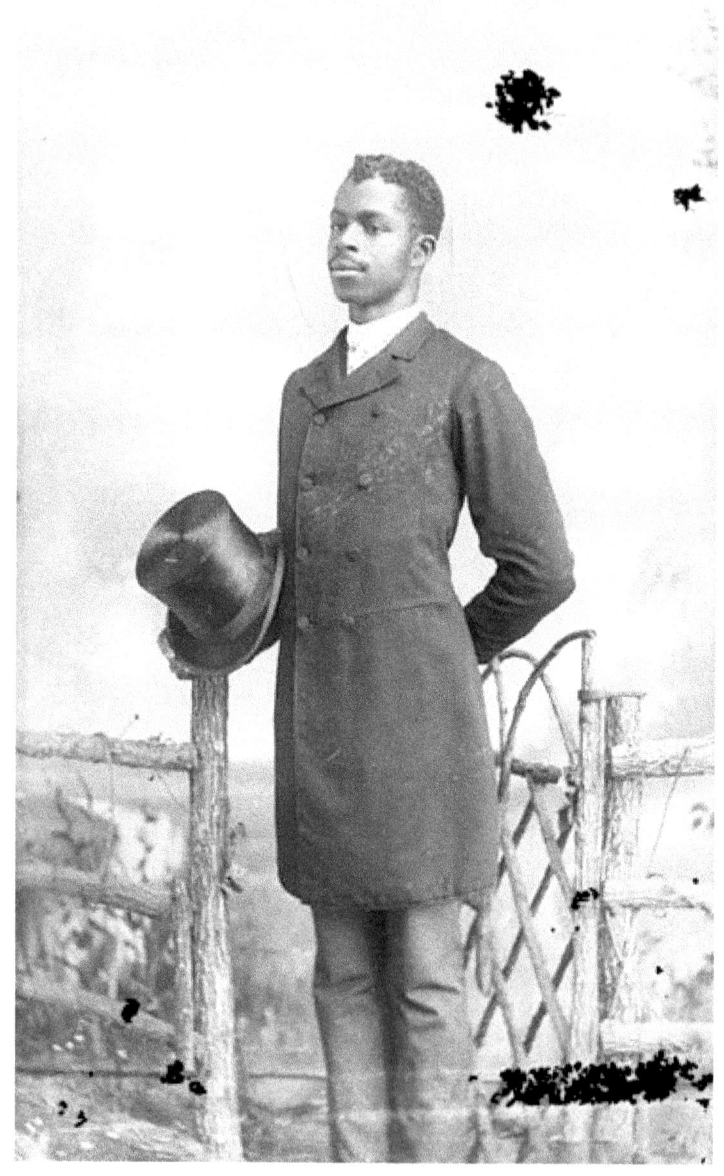

Angels are chimaeras of our desire for control over the apparently random senseless sequence of events that characterize our everyday lives.

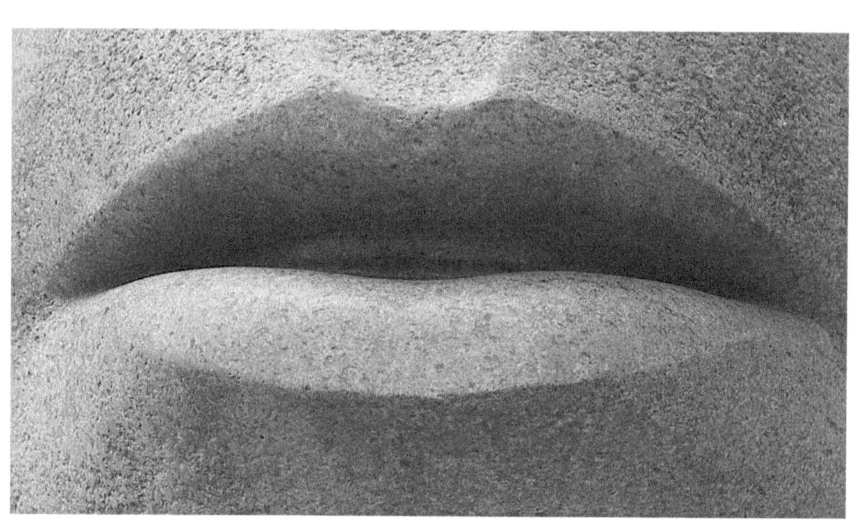

If praying for angels is the only hope, there is no hope. Praying is whining, a pressure valve release, a slow hiss of deflating egos.

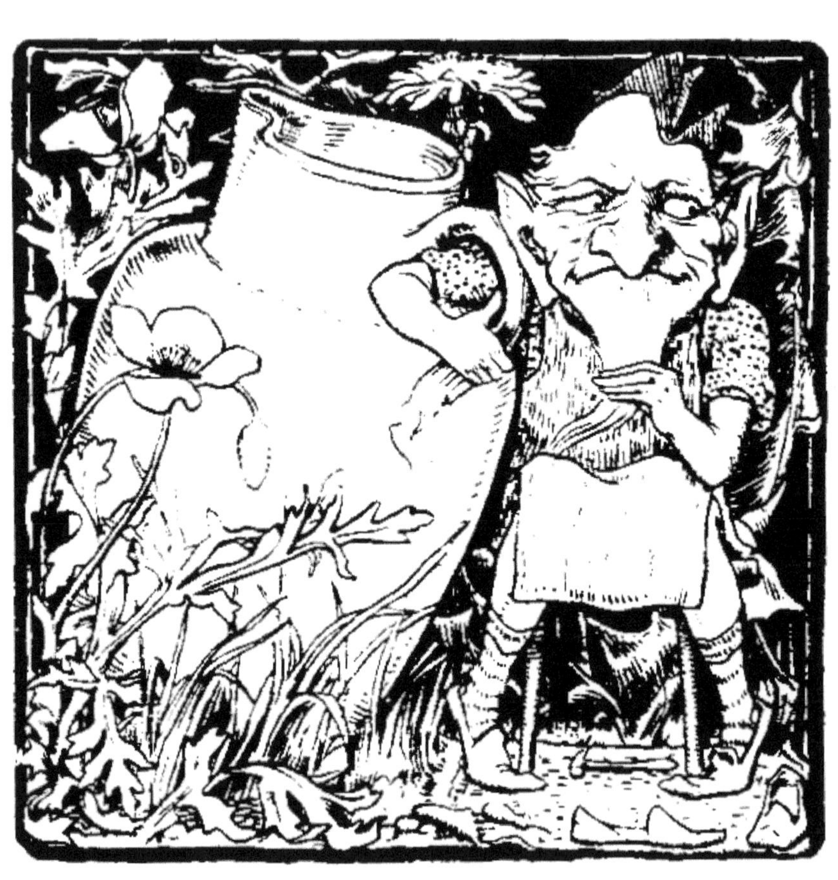

We are inundated with stories telling us that wishing and hoping can get you what you want. However, even in the early stories of angels, genies and little people who grant wishes, the wish fulfilled rarely brings satisfaction or happiness. The angel seems to trick the wisher and perhaps this is the point.

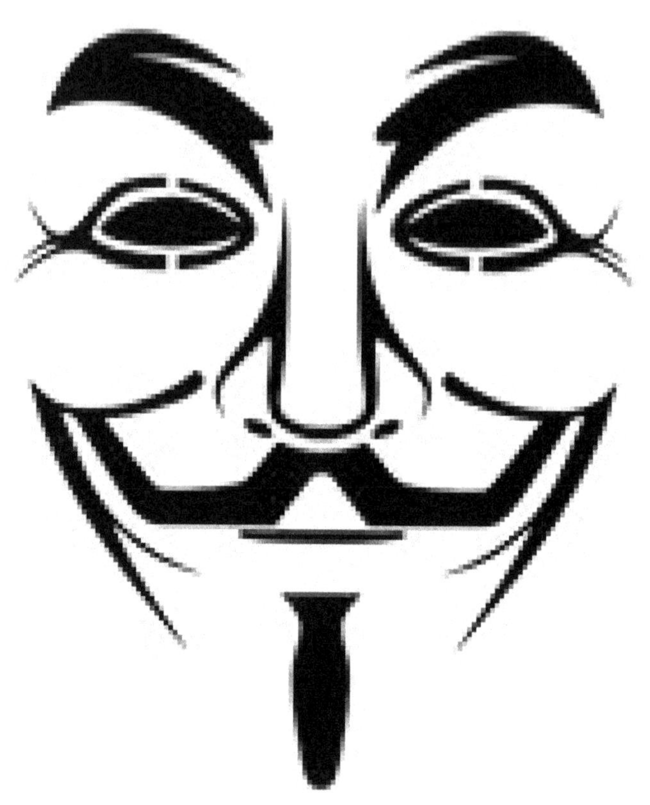

Those who believe in the
holiness of the virgin are
lost, they have missed the
apocalypse, the beast has come
and they are living in it.

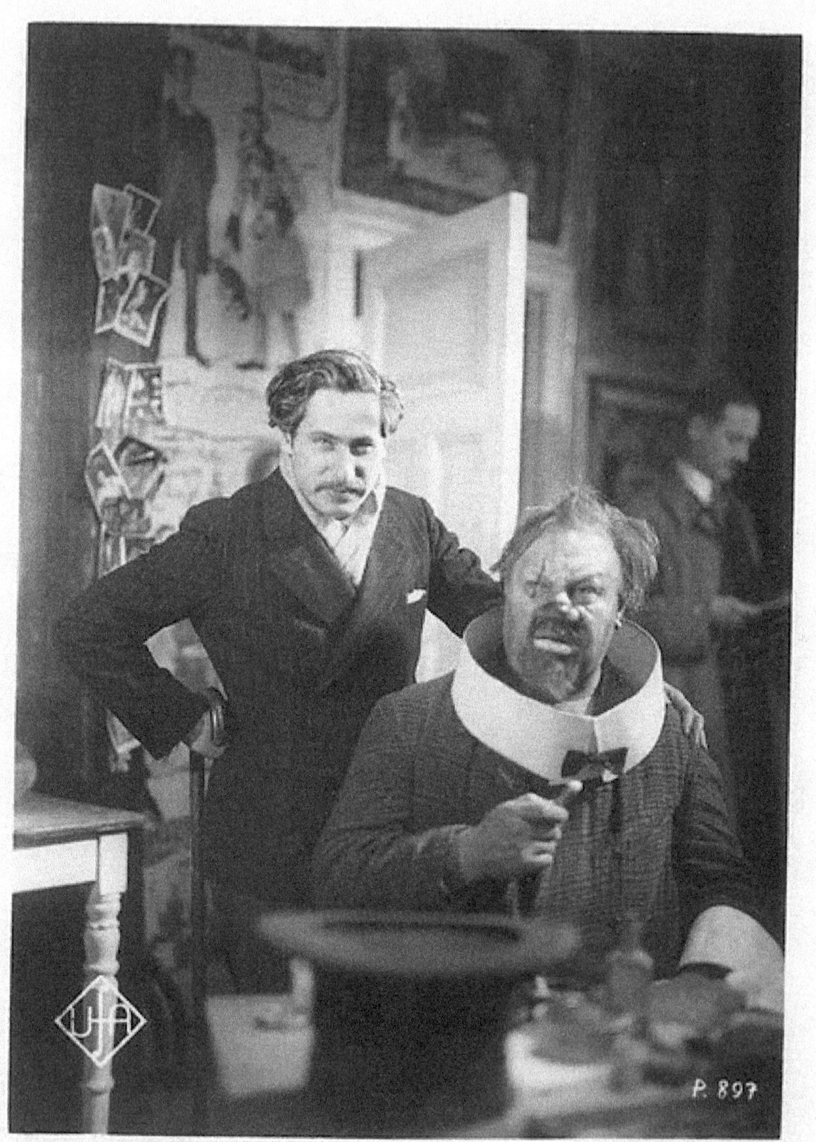
P. 897

The return of angels is only a metaphysical heartburn, a repetition of the spirit at the beginning of spiritlessness, a memory of a belief in the era of the unbelievable. The angel returns as an image of supernatural power in the context of growing powerlessness.

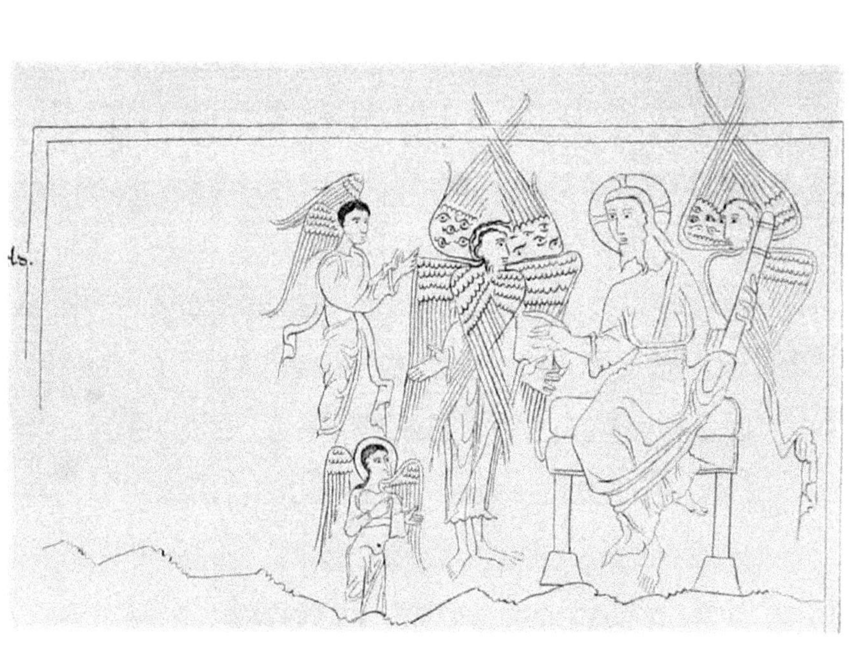

# REVENGE

In fact, the revenge of angels, inspired by our insipid whining, could in fact be the cause of evil. Angels are acting as hired bullies, vigilantes, meting out rough justice upon unsuspecting transgressors unsure of what we have accused them of: not paying enough attention to us or whatever.

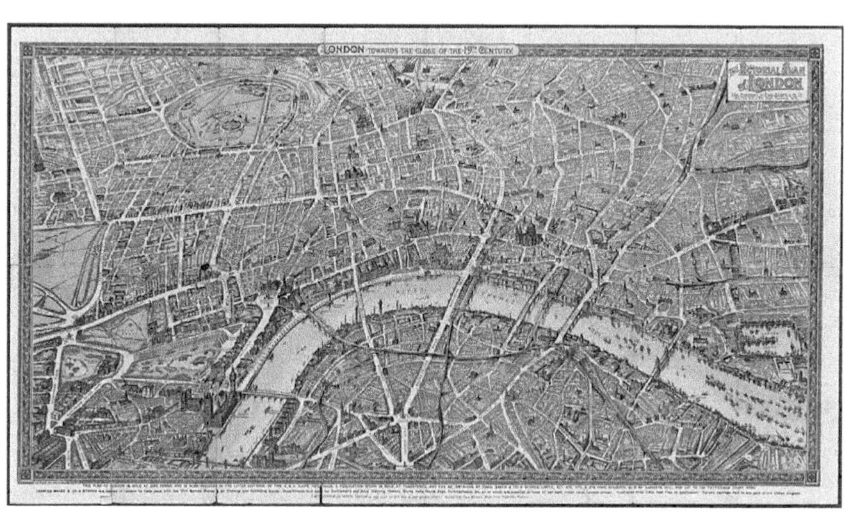
LONDON TOWARDS THE CLOSE OF THE 19TH CENTURY
LONDON

Whatever that resistance, that allows us to talk about walking on water but never lets us experience it, is called, be it nature or whatever, begs for the existence of some animating force to intervene on our behalf.

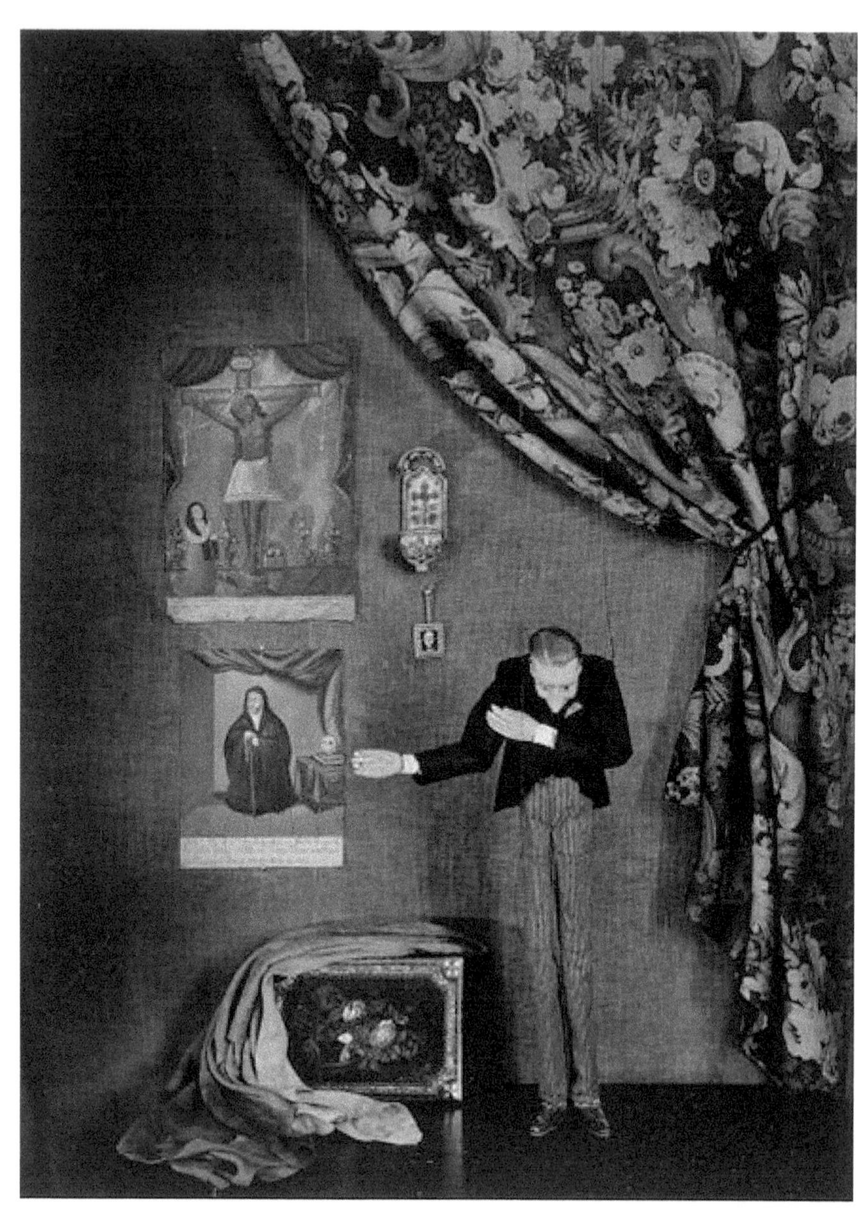

Like the trickster, technology is devious. It seems to allow us to overcome the ravages of some disease while creating another one, or just giving us enough life to fully feel the ravages of old age. Our pleadings for revenge against the endless dreariness are met with the revenge of angels.

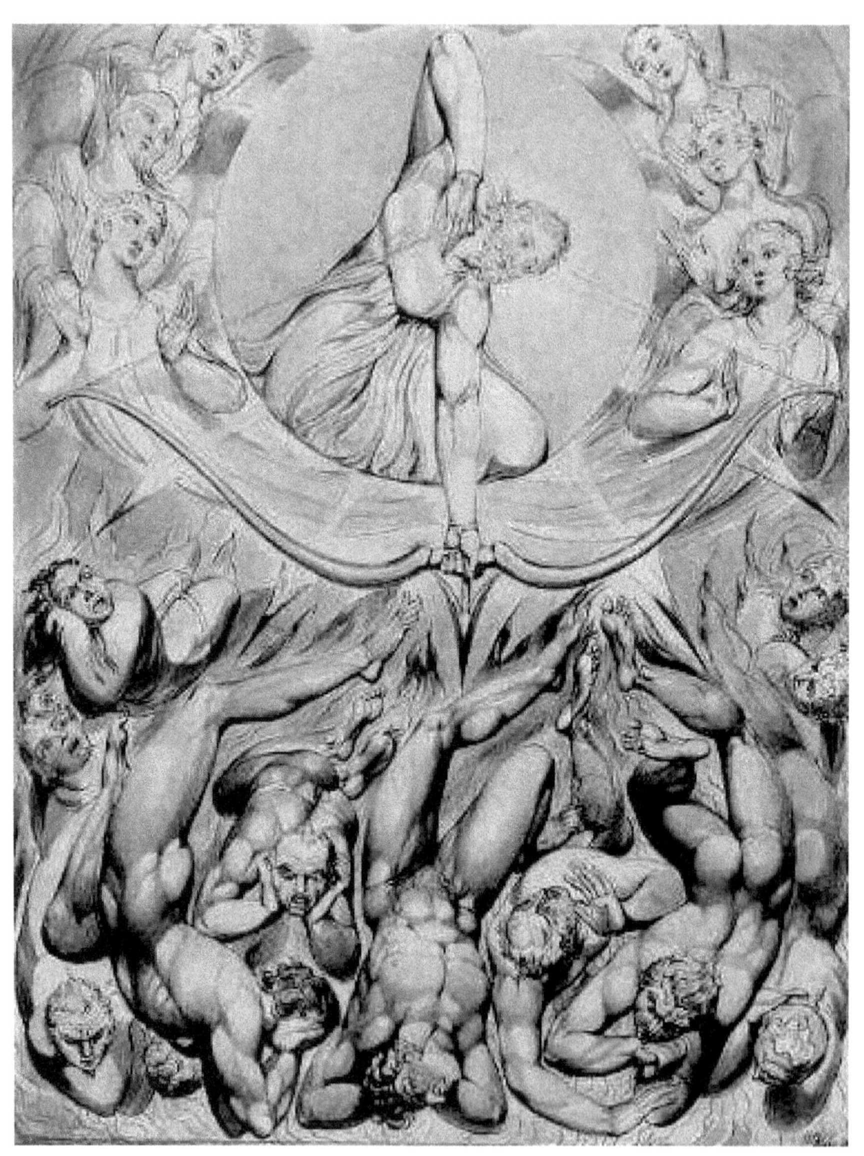

# FALLEN ANGELS

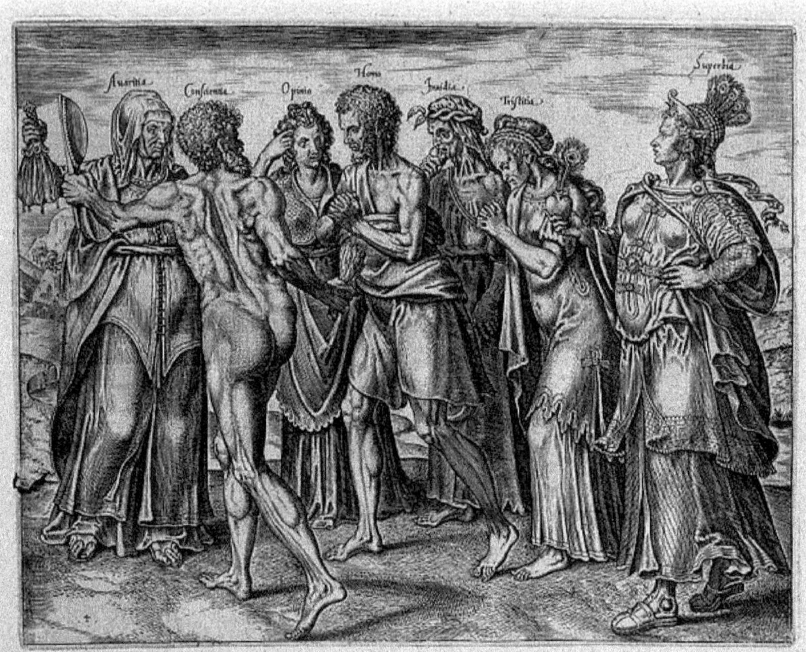


Nempe mala occulto stabulant grauiora recessu
Intus: ibi fastus, mœror, liuorque malignus,
Turpis auaritia, ac persuasio credula, mensque
Conscia, crudeli distringunt pectora plaga.

Dit sijn noch al niet dan wtwendighe plaghen
Draghen een vroom hert lijdsamelijck inne vreught:
Maer binnen quelt der conscientien knaghen
Door-ghierichèyt/ hooghmoet/ nijt ende onghenueght.

*Or tous ces maux ne font qu'extreme dueil*
*Qu'vn cueur fidele endure en patience:*
*Mais le Remors l'ame afflige à outrance,*
*Par Auarice, Enuie, & triste Orgueil.*

IIII

Every hero of substantial promise is ultimately the purveyor of pain. Every angel is only the image of our desire but is also the substance of our suffering.

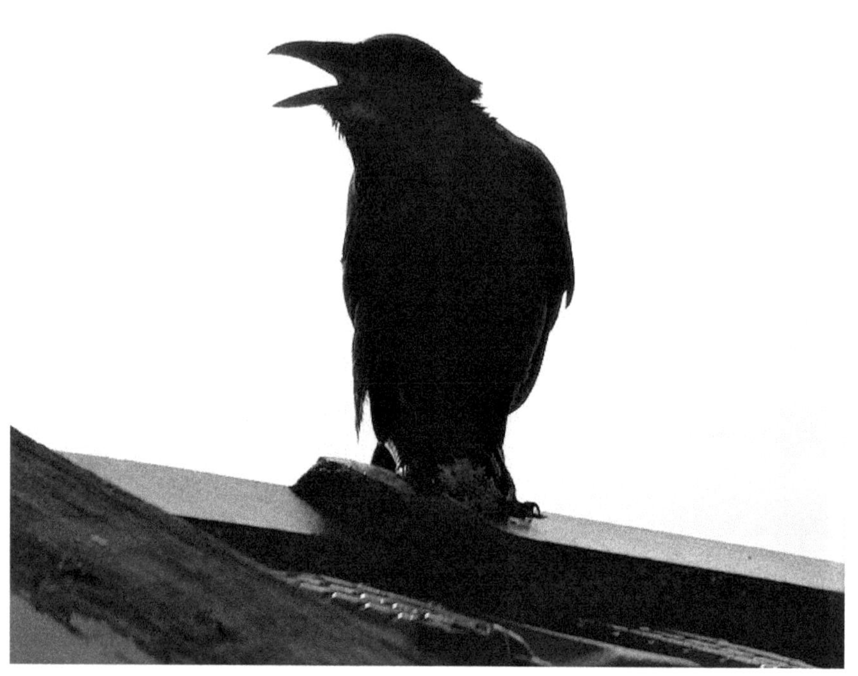

Until now, art, which could simulate great beauty or represent intensity and passion was ultimately a tease, a pornography if you will, demanding consummation but never allowing it. Look but don't touch.

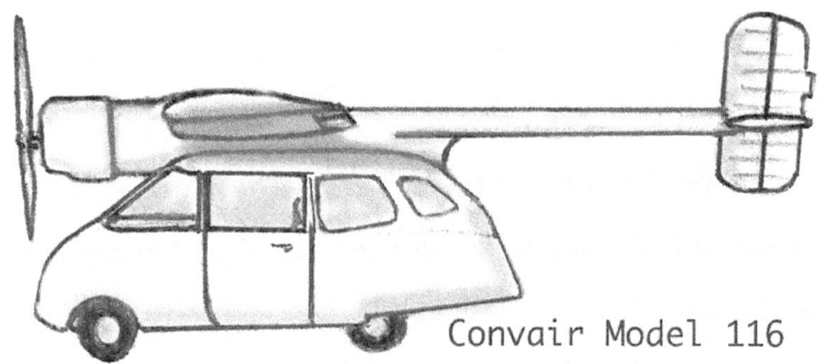

Convair Model 116

Apparently we now stand at the brink of the possibility of passing through the looking glass, of fantasy machines simulating physical sensation.

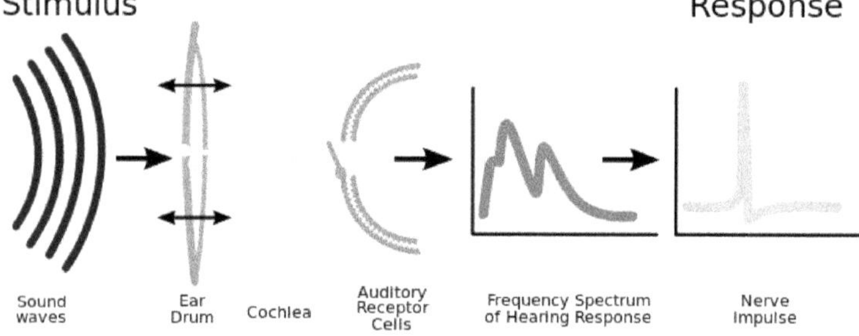
Stimulus
Response
Sound waves
Ear Drum
Cochlea
Auditory Receptor Cells
Frequency Spectrum of Hearing Response
Nerve Impulse

When the line between virtual sex and fucking becomes as indecipherably thin as the difference between digital reproduction and actual sound, will our escapes from boredom become as unimaginative as our lives?

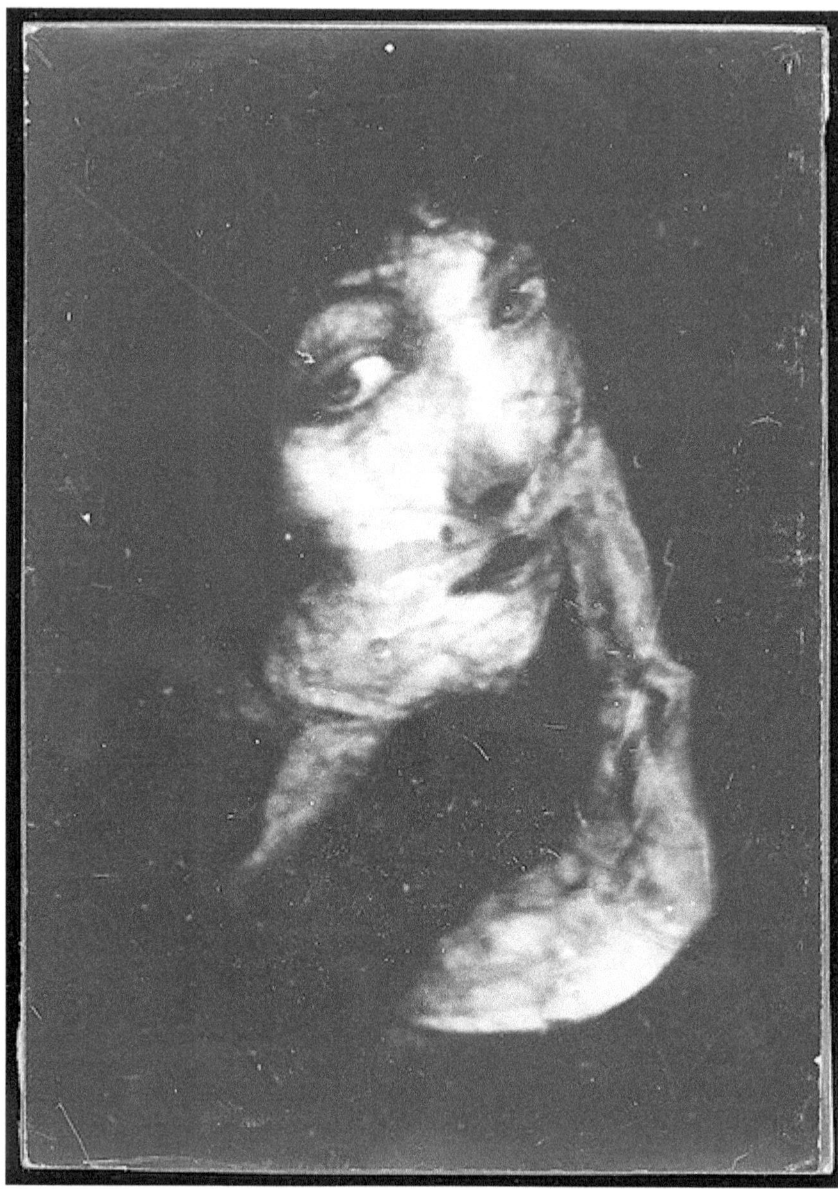

Perhaps the question itself is redundant since the distinction between our 'real' tedium and our 'artificial' tedium is unnecessarily sanctified. The romanticization of so-called real sex, whether sex in marriage, sex with love, or sex with a body, is only a pretext for the shame we feel about our fantasies: our simulated sex.

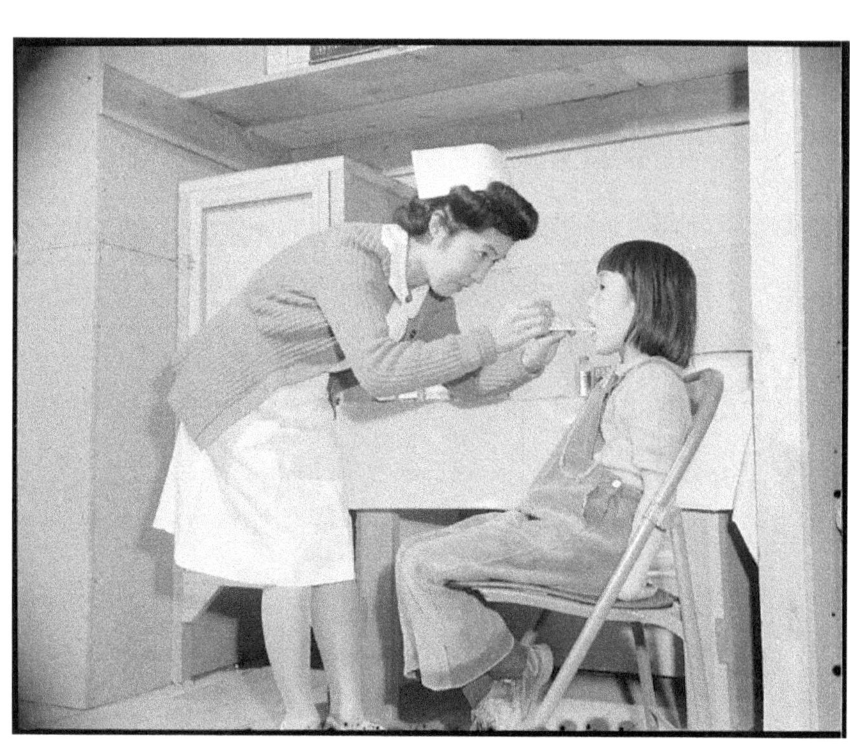

The difference may be important only to those pompous enough to accept the limitations of their own imaginations.

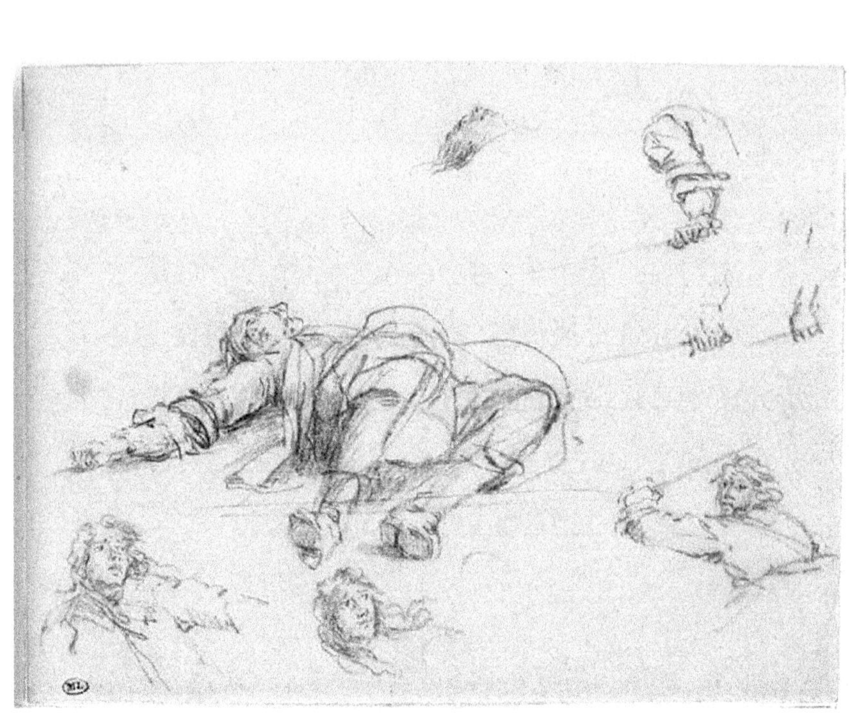

The separation of thought and experience will no longer hold in the era of technological mysticism. The communication network subverts the distinctions between public and private, interior and exterior.

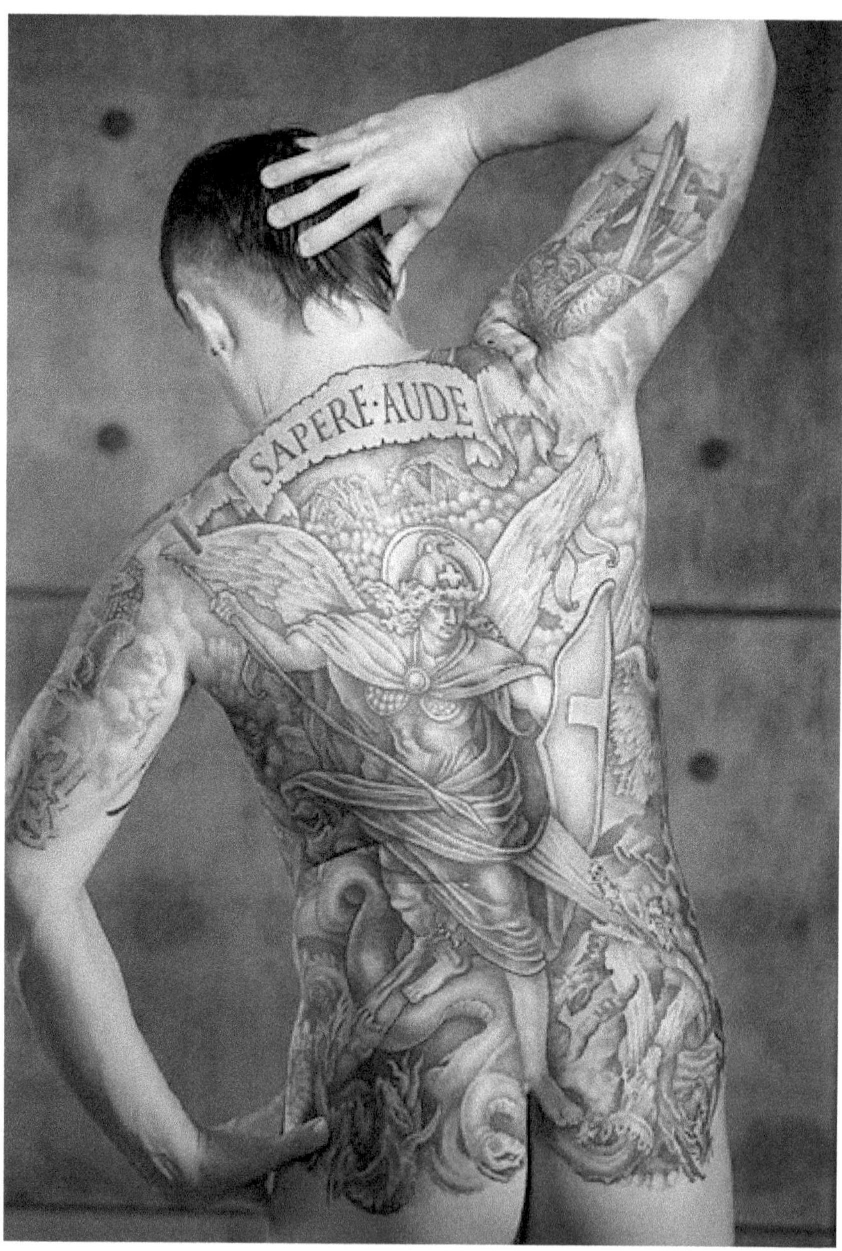
SAPERE·AUDE

In this context, the obscene dominates: the penetration of bodies with organs, weapons and tools. The pierced body is the emblem of this condition, that and the never ending confessional of contemporary life, where every indiscretion and personality defect is punished and major violations are sources of amusement.

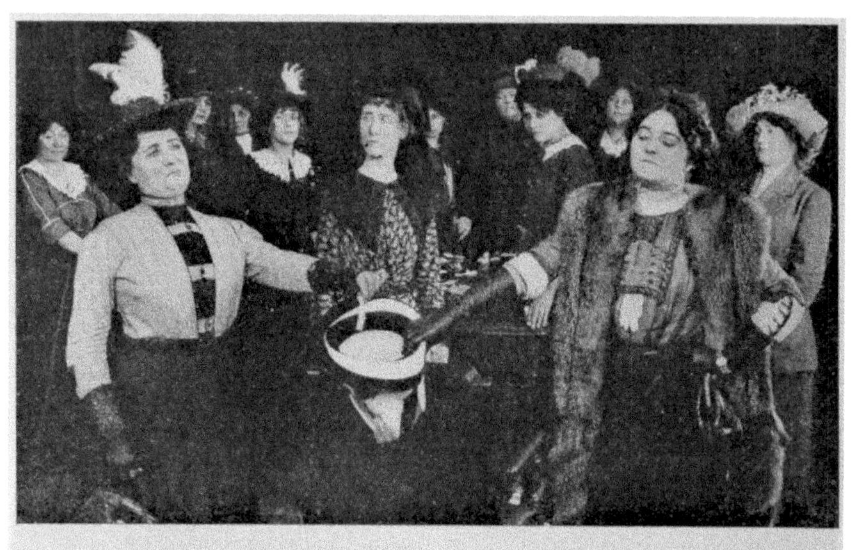

BALLOTING IN THE JURY-ROOM

Our worth is measured in our capacity to reveal, our ability to stand naked and the relish with which we testify to our desires.

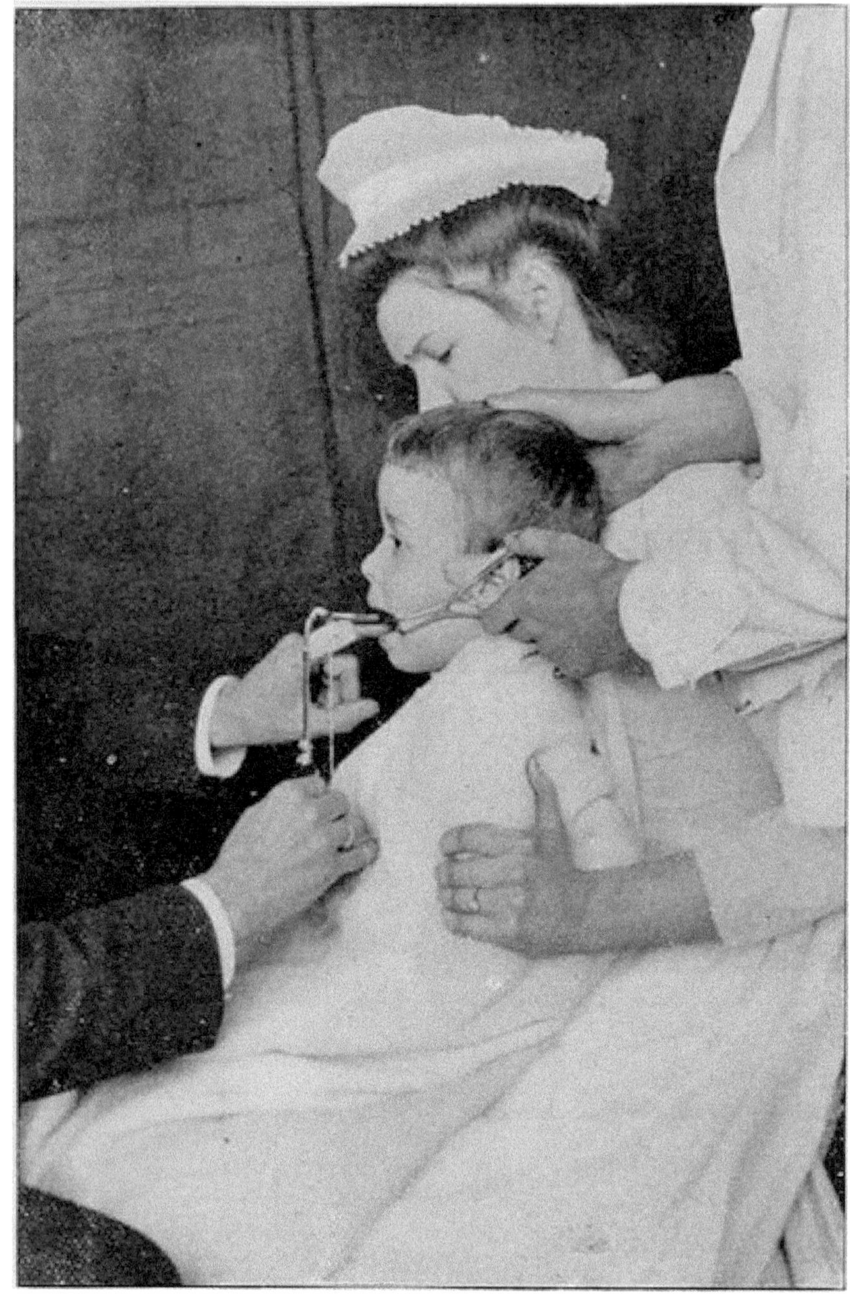

"The need to speak, even if one has nothing to say, becomes more pressing when one has nothing to say, just as the will to live becomes more urgent when life has lost its meaning."
--Jean Baudrillard

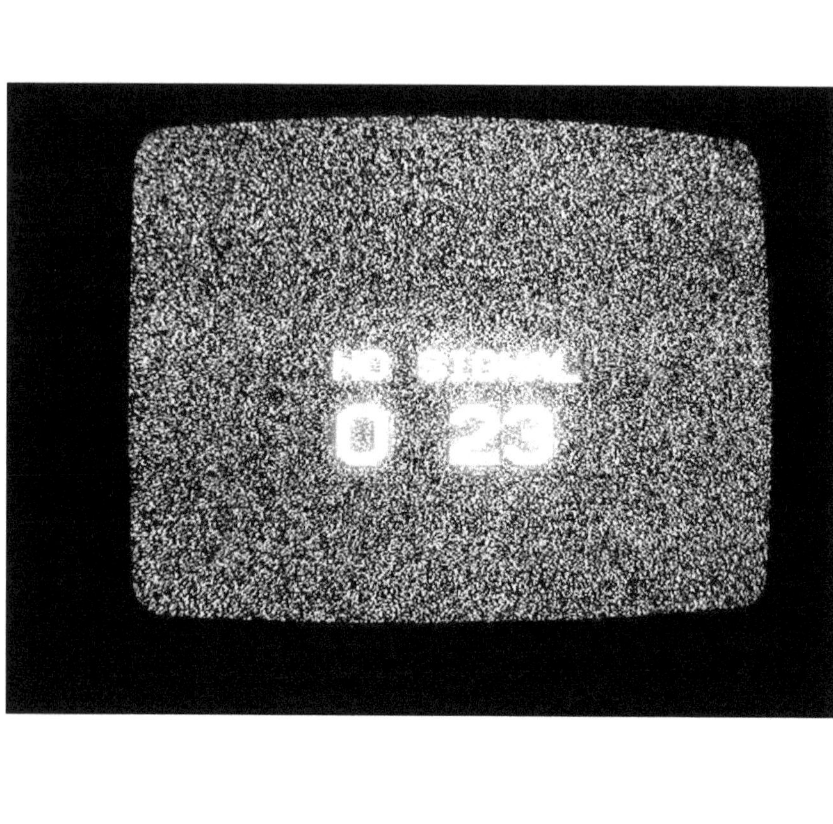
0 23

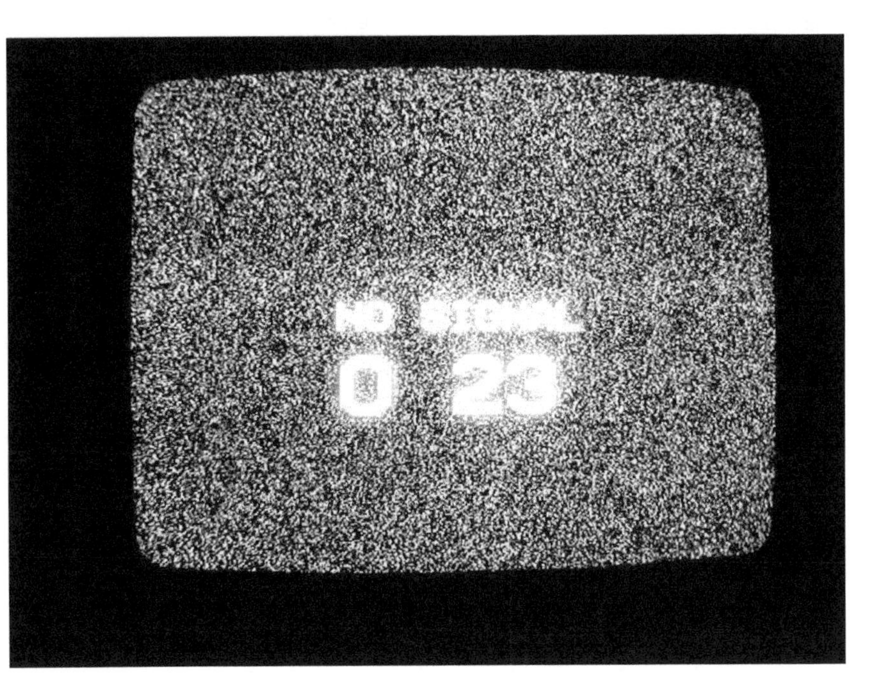
NO SIGNAL
0 23

# Post Scriptum

This book is based on a video installation created by Greg Thompson and Donal McGraith presented under the pseudonym Domhnaill O'Cearnachain for an exhibition called *The Angel Show* held at Artspace in Peterborough, Ontario, Canada from September 9 to November 5, 1994. It included work by Dominic Hardy, Calla Shea, and Chris Hardwicke. It also included a performance by David Bateman. *Angel Day Turning* was a video installation placed in a kind of confessional where one person at a time could sit and watch the video. Pretty much everything about the installation was amateurish and showed little talent. A rather pathetic piece not worthy of being in the same room with some rather finely crafted pieces by the actual artists named above.

I have endeavoured to improve the presentation of the work in the faint hope that some modicum of meaning has been achieved by this new way of presenting it. All that remains from the original is the text, which is unchanged. All the images are changed to suit a new conception of the piece. While this too will fail, even less people will be disappointed as other than myself and my friend no one will see it.

To further expand the self-pity in this statement: "If a tree falls in a forest and no one is around the hear it, does it make a sound?"

# Illustrations

The images used are Creative Commons images taken from Wikimedia Commons. They are either in the public domain or made available under various Creative Commons licenses. The license links follow. I have also included the URL of each image location in case additional information about any image is sought.

Links to licenses:
CC0 1.0 Universal (CC0 1.0) Public Domain Dedication
https://creativecommons.org/publicdomain/zero/1.0/deed.en
Creative Commons Attribution 2.0 Generic (CC BY 2.0)
https://creativecommons.org/licenses/by/2.0/deed.en
Creative Commons Attribution-ShareAlike 2.0 Generic (CC BY-SA 2.0)
https://creativecommons.org/licenses/by-sa/2.0/deed.en
Creative Commons Attribution 2.5 Generic (CC BY 2.5)
https://creativecommons.org/licenses/by/2.5/deed.en
Creative Commons Attribution- ShareAlike 2.5 Generic (CC BY-SA 2.5)
https://creativecommons.org/licenses/by-sa/2.5/deed.en
Creative Commons Attribution-ShareAlike 3.0 Unported (CC BY-SA 3.0)
https://creativecommons.org/licenses/by-sa/3.0/deed.en
Creative Commons Attribution 4.0 International (CC BY 4.0)
https://creativecommons.org/licenses/by/4.0/deed.en
Creative Commons Attribution-ShareAlike 4.0 International (CC BY-SA 4.0)
https://creativecommons.org/licenses/by-sa/4.0/deed.en

page 6
From Project Gutenberg's The Life-Story of Insects, by Geo. H. Carpenter, Public Domain. https://commons.wikimedia.org/wiki/File:Common_Cockroach_-_Project_Gutenberg_eText_16410.png
page 8
Page 845 from journal Die Gartenlaube for 1863, Public Domain. https://commons.wikimedia.org/wiki/File:Die_Gartenlaube_(1863)_845.jpg
page 10
Unknown Photographer, Public Domain. https://commons.wikimedia.org/wiki/File:Theda_Bara_publicity_card_1916.jpg
page 12
Unknown Photographer, Public Domain. https://commons.wikimedia.org/wiki/File:La_jeune_fille_et_l%27oiseau_(1900).jpg
page 14
W.A. Jones, Public Domain. https://commons.wikimedia.org/wiki/File:StateLibQld_2_139795_Young_woman_wearing_a_skirt_and_striped_cardigan,_reclining_on_a_chair_for_a_studio_portrait,_1940-1950.jpg
page 16
E.B. & E.C. Kellogg (Firm), Public Domain. https://commons.wikimedia.org/wiki/File:EB%26EC_Kellogg_Brothers,_Illustrative_Map_of_Human_Life,_1847_Cornell_CUL_PJM_1054_01.jpg

page 18
Wilhelm von Gloeden, Public Domain. https://commons.wikimedia.org/w/index.php?curid=3538800
page 20
Pat Loika, CC BY 2.0 (link above) The original colour photograph has been changed to black and white. https://commons.wikimedia.org/wiki/File:Long_Beach_Comic_Con_2012_- _Freddy_Krueger_(8156403650).jpg
page 22
Albrecht Dürer, Public Domain. https://commons.wikimedia.org/wiki/File:Albrecht_D%C3%Bcrer_-_The_Four_Avenging_Angels _(NGA_1971.39.6).jpg
page 24
wpclipart.com, Public Domain. https://commons.wikimedia.org/wiki/File:Sign_language_Y.svg
page 26
UPC for Spool CD, permission for reproduction granted by owner, 2020
page 28
Araujojoan96, CC BY-SA 3.0 (link above) The original colour photograph has been changed to black and white. https://commons.wikimedia.org/wiki/File:Silhouettes-legs.JPG
page 30
Fortepan ID 253, Adományozó/Donor: Fortepan. CC BY-SA 3.0 (link above) https://commons.wikimedia.org/wiki/File:Double_portrait,_women,_twins,_beach,_deck_chair,_sunshades_Fortepan_253.jpg
page 32
Earnest Edgar Strathy Smith, City of Toronto Archives, CC BY 2.0 (link above) https://commons.wikimedia.org/wiki/File:PCC_streetcar_4107_on_Queen_Street_East.jpg
page 34
Rasheedhrasheed, CC BY-SA 4.0 (link above)
https://commons.wikimedia.org/wiki/File:Beautiful_Seashell.jpg
page 36
Wilhelm von Gloeden, Public Domain. https://commons.wikimedia.org/wiki/File:Gloeden,_Wilhelm_von_(1856-1931)_-_n._0679_B_- _Timbrata_-_da_-_%27Po%C3%A9sies_arcadiennes%27.jpg
page 38
G. Plüschow, File from Welcome Collection, CC BY 4.0 (link above) https://commons.wikimedia.org/wiki/File:A_Sicilian_boy,_posing_naked_outdoors,_by_a_door_Wellcome_L0034525.jpg
page 40
Titus 36, edit by Cornischong at lb.wikipedia, CC BY-SA 2.5 (link above) This image has been change to black and white.
https://commons.wikimedia.org/w/index.php?curid=19505254
page 42
Trailer screenshot (MGM), Public Domain.
https://commons.wikimedia.org/wiki/File:Robert_Warwick_%26_Joan_Crawford_in_A_Woman%27s_Face_trailer.jpg
page 44
File from Welcome Images, CC BY 4.0 (link above)

https://commons.wikimedia.org/w/index.php?curid=36027336
page 46
Egon Schiele, Public Domain. https://commons.wikimedia.org/wiki/File:Egon_Schiele_-_Seated_Woman_with_Legs_Drawn_Up_(Adele_Herms)_-_Google_Art_Project.jpg
page 48
Unknown Photographer, Stockholm Transport Museum Commons, Public Domain. https://commons.wikimedia.org/wiki/File:Aftermath_of_the_second_world_war._Shop_window_in_London_1946_(6334338904).jpg
page 50
Jan Luyken, Public Domain. https://commons.wikimedia.org/w/index.php?curid=3750406
page 52
Photo from Patafisik and Elena Tartaglione, Public Domain. https://commons.wikimedia.org/wiki/File:Automa_Manzetti_1840.JPG
page 54
Pearson Scott Foresman, Public Domain. https://commons.wikimedia.org/wiki/File:Apex_(PSF).png
page 56
Rainer Gerhards, CC BY-SA 3.0 (link above) The original colour image has been changed to black and white.
https://commons.wikimedia.org/wiki/File:Punch-card-cobol.jpg
page 58
Egon Schiele, Public Domain. https://commons.wikimedia.org/wiki/File:Schiele_-_Kauernde.jpg
page 60
Unknown Photographer, Public Domain. https://commons.wikimedia.org/wiki/File:Peoples_Gas_Building,_Chicago,_is_one_of_Chicago%27s_most_modern_skyscrapers,_stands_out_very..._(NBY_415929).jpg
page 62
Basile Morin, CC BY-SA 4.0 (link above) The original image has been cropped.
https://commons.wikimedia.org/wiki/File:Sculptures_of_god_Shiva_dancing_Thandavam.jpg
page 64
Charles Jay Taylor, Puck Magazine, Public Domain.
https://commons.wikimedia.org/wiki/File:TINMAN4.jpg
page 66
Wilhelm von Gloeden, Public Domain. https://commons.wikimedia.org/wiki/File:Gloeden,_Wilhelm_von_(1856-1931)_-_n._2071.jpg
page 68
Martin Schongauer, Cleveland Museum of Art, Dudley P. Allen Fund, CC0 1.0 (link above) https://commons.wikimedia.org/wiki/File:Martin_Schongauer_-_The_Angel_of_the_Annunciation_-_1958.173_-_Cleveland_Museum_of_Art.jpg
page 70
Metro Pictures Corporation, Public Domain.
https://commons.wikimedia.org/wiki/File:Satan_Junior_(1919)_-_Ad_1.jpg
page 72

ABC Television, Public Domain. https://commons.wikimedia.org/wiki/File:Eartha_Kitt_Catwoman_Batman_1967.JPG
page 74
Street & Smith Corp., Picture Play Magazine, Public Domain. https://commons.wikimedia.org/wiki/File:Marie_Provost_in_%22The_Beautiful_and_Damned%22_(Jan._1923).png
page 76
Eadweard Muybridge, Public Domain.
https://commons.wikimedia.org/wiki/File:Nude_man_doing_a_handspring_over_another_nude_man%27s_back_(rbm-QP301M8-1887-364a~6).jpg
page 78
The Sydney Mail, Public Domain. https://commons.wikimedia.org/wiki/File:Crossing_of_Blue_Mountains,_1880.jpg
page 80
Walter Crane, Public Domain. https://commons.wikimedia.org/wiki/File:Medusa_Head_Drawing.jpg
page 82
Alvan S. Harper, Public Domain. https://commons.wikimedia.org/wiki/File:Man_holding_a_top_hat_(3248110198).jpg
page 84
Kobolt, Imported from 500px by the Archive Team, CC BY-SA 3.0 (link above)
https://commons.wikimedia.org/wiki/File:Lips_(55208584).jpeg
page 86
T.C. Kroker, Public Domain. https://commons.wikimedia.org/wiki/File:Leprechaun_or_Clurichaun.png
page 88
Cleslie92, CC BY-SA 3.0 (link above) https://commons.wikimedia.org/wiki/File:PROGRESSFaceless.jpg
page 90
Paramount Pictures, Josef von Sternberg, Public Domain. https://commons.wikimedia.org/wiki/File:The_Blue_Angel_(film)_1930_BW_photo_on_set,_Josef_von_Sternberg_(director),_Emil_Jannings.jpg
page 92
Stephen Humphrey Villiers Gurteen, Public Domain. https://commons.wikimedia.org/wiki/File:The_epic_of_the_fall_of_man;_a_comparative_study_of_Caedmon,_Dante_and_Milton_(1896)_(14802914913).jpg
page 94
William Pina, CC BY-SA 3.0 (link above) The original image has been cropped.
https://commons.wikimedia.org/wiki/File:TV_Static.jpg
page 96
London, Charles Baker & Co., Public Domain. https://commons.wikimedia.org/wiki/File:1890s_pictorial_map_of_London_-_London_towards_the_close_of_the_19th_century.jpg
page 98
Tina Modotti, Houston Museum of Fine Arts, Public Domain. https://commons.wikimedia.org/wiki/File:Tina_Modotti_-_Rene_d%27Harnoncourt_Puppet_- _Google_Art_Project.jpg
page 100
William Blake, Public Domain.

https://commons.wikimedia.org/wiki/
File:William_Blake,_The_Casting_of_the_Rebel_Angels_into_Hell.JPG
page 102
Engraving by P. Galle, Welcome Images, CC BY 4.0 (link above) The original coloured image has been changed to black and white.
https://commons.wikimedia.org/wiki/File:A_man_prays_to_Conscience,_
represented_by_a_naked_man;_figur_Wellcome_V0007587.jpg
page 104
Sardaka, CC BY-SA 4.0 (link above) The original colour image has been changed to black and white. https://commons.wikimedia.org/
wiki/File:(1)Crow_on_roof-1.jpg
page 106
Bzuk (talk), CC0 1.0 (link above) https://commons.wikimedia.org/wiki/
File:Convair_Model_116_drawing.jpg
page 108
Original diagram by Tim Gollisch, Andreas M. V. Herz, and Public Library of Science. Converted to SVG by Iain 03:57, 12 June 2006 (UTC) CC BY-SA 2.5 (link above) Original image has been changed to black and white.
https://commons.wikimedia.org/wiki/File:Processing-of-sound.svg
page 110
Gustave Geley, CC0 1.0 (link above) https://commons.wikimedia.org/wiki/File:-
Materialization_of_a_Woman
%27s_Face_Produced_by_the_Medium_Eva_C.-_MET_DP71232.jpg
page 112
Tom Parker, Public Domain. https://commons.wikimedia.org/wiki/
File:Granada_Relocation_Center,_Amache,_Colorado._The_school_nurse_administers_a_throat_swabbing_to_a_yo_._._._-_NARA_-_539056.jpg
page 114
Adam Frans van der Meulen, Public Domain.
https://commons.wikimedia.org/wiki/File:Adam_Frans_van_der_Meulen_-
_Dead_soldier,_three_half_figures_fighting,_three_hands_holding_a_sword.jpg
page 116
Tatoo: Anton Ivkin, Photographer: Alexander Kuzovlev, CC BY-SA 4.0 (link above) https://commons.wikimedia.org/wiki/File:Man_with_a_full_back_
Christian_and_Enlightenment_tattoo._Black_and_White.jpg
page 118
The Motion Picture Story Magazine, Public Domain. https://commons.
wikimedia.org/wiki/File:The_First_Woman_Jury_in_America_02.png
page 120
Louis Starr and Thompson S. Westcott, An American Text-book of the diseases of children, Public Domain.
https://commons.wikimedia.org/wiki/File:An_American_text-
book_of_the_diseases_of_children_(1895)_(14802229383).jpg
page 122
Liz Sullivan, CC BY-SA 4.0 (link above) The original image has been cropped.
https://commons.wikimedia.org/w/index.php?curid=35287591

www.ingramcontent.com/pod-product-compliance
Ingram Content Group UK Ltd.
Pitfield, Milton Keynes, MK11 3LW, UK
UKHW020423250726
13967UKWH00007B/2787